THE OTHER 99 T.Y.M.E.S

Train Your Mind to Enjoy Serenity

Million Dollar Pen, Ink.

Sometimes, we spend so much time focusing on the one thing that went wrong; we lose sight of the 99 other times things went right.

THE OTHER

99

TRAIN

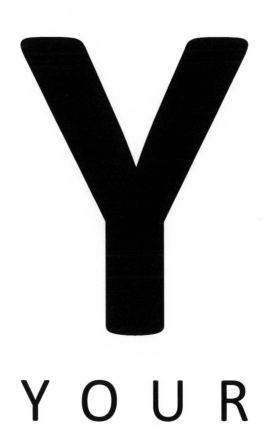

YOUR

MIND

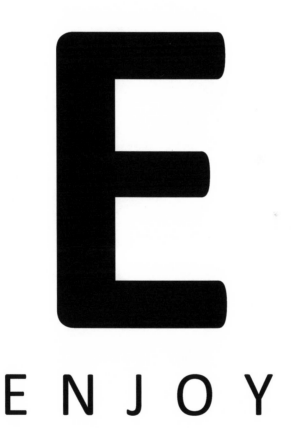

ENJOY

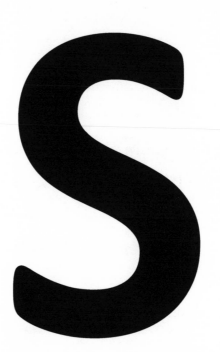

SERENITY

TABLE OF CONTENTS

The best experiences in life should leave an indelible impression on one's memory.

The truth will, with certainty, lay the character of men and women bare. Do not be fooled by perception. Be persuaded by facts.

While you are bragging about all the things you plan to do, others are busy accomplishing everything they've been planning.

It is never wise to offend or take advantage of a benefactor. The generosity of a mentor, business partner or company can potentially flow in abundance when appreciated and will surely be depleted if abused.

FOREWORD

RALPH WALDO EMERSON once said that in order to achieve content-ment, one should "cultivate the habit of being grateful for every good thing that comes to you, and to give thanks continuously." Researchers have found that the act of counting one's blessings actually helps strengthen relationships, in all forms. However, not everyone understands the signif-icance of putting the behavior into practice. In *"The Other 99 T.Y.M.E.S"* the undervalued concept of gratitude is the critical theme which defines the groundbreaking sophomore narrative by Carlos Wallace, author of the bestseller *"Life Is Not Complicated, You Are."* Thanks to Wallace's signature style of using relatable, salient life experiences he is able to draw readers into accepting realities they may otherwise avoid and offer them alternative, positive ways to view life's challenges. Each chapter is written with such searing honesty and generous substance, **99** is des-tined to become the singular most important guide in the life of anyone seeking the true meaning of gratitude. While many people claim they've experienced the quality or feeling of being grateful, truth of the matter is the sentiment is often driven by circumstances (mostly favorable) which elicit one's deep appreciation. Most times, when faced with unfavorable conditions we have a difficult time finding a reason to be thankful. Most people find the prospect of overlooking an occasional affront, injustice or challenge rather daunting. The propensity to harp on the negative is so habitual they are oblivious to the moments where life actually worked out. Fewer still will accept that treasuring one's blessings can actually counteract the effects of a bad experiences.

This may all be an enigmatic concept for some to grasp; the realization that although you have hit some rough patches that should never negate moments that a kind word, a caring act, an instance of forgiveness or the rewarding feeling of knowing you worked hard to achieve a goal satisfied you and made you happy.

In order to understand the reasoning behind Wallace's concept of valuing the virtues of gratitude, one must first understand the author.

When I first met Carlos Wallace, author of the international best-selling book *"**Life Is Not Complicated, You Are**"*, ironically (and this was long before the title of his first effort was ever conceived) I summed up the man's character in one word: Complicated. Safe to say, talking and working with Carlos as a comic and later as a publicist for his record breaking "Top Dogs of Comedy" tour was, in a word, intense. As I reflect on our initial interaction I still maintain that getting to know Carlos has been an experience unlike any other.

Having studied psychology for a brief period in college, I was versed in the psychological determinants of behavior: phrases like Type-A personality and terms such as ego and superego. The lexicon is often applied by lay people (in terms of non-clinical attributions) to describe men and women with personalities so pragmatic, so dominant and so un-yielding they are extremely difficult to relate to. While the latter proved a complete misnomer with regard to Carlos Wallace, the former depictions are spot on. The author and professor is not only a dominant figure, he possesses the strategic, practical and fiercely determined mind that, if you look carefully at leaders described throughout history, places him in a position of extraordinary company. One has only to spend a single day with the man as he prepares for a sold-out comedy event, plans a strategy meeting with his artists and staff, prepares for a presentation with the

President of Lone Star College, gathers his thoughts and ideas for a television or radio interview or transcribes notes for his new book, *"The Other 99 T.Y.M.E.S"* and you will realize (if you pay close enough attention) this is a mind that is constantly at work. Carlos Wallace literally thinks with machine like precision. One can even call the man prescient to a certain degree, given his uncanny ability to think and make decisions several steps ahead of any situation. And in the midst of this process, or perhaps as a direct result, distractions are not only unwanted, they sepa-rate from his pragmatic demeanor like oil over water; they never merge. It is chemically impossible for the properties to mix. And in the case of an individual who is in a constant state of forward momentum, distractions become lost in the physics of thought and action; they are left hanging in a past moment that no longer interests him because he has already made use of that time and has moved on to another thought, another idea, another phase of his growth. Time does not stand still. Neither does Wallace. As he noted in *"Life Is Not Complicated, You Are"*, challenges and negativity should become a catalyst to success. Readers will learn in *"The Other 99 T.Y.M.E.S"*, they should never be forethought. To preoc-cupy one's mind, one's heart with all the times someone hurt you means you leave no room to appreciate all the other times that person comfort-ed you or made you smile. If you concentrate so deeply on the negative factors you are unable to acknowledge all the positive results. Ultimately, you simply lose sight of what really matters in life.

As the founder of Million$Pen, Ink. and editor and creative con-sultant of *"Life Is Not Complicated, You Are"*, we were thrilled when Carlos hired our company to help with his first literary effort. We were also cautious in our approach. This is not a client that should be taken lightly. His demands are great, his expectations high and his work ethic impeccable. So we did what we do with every client. We studied his routine. We familiarized ourselves with the complexities of his thought process. We researched, reviewed and committed our-selves to relating the second part of his amazing story to the masses. In the process, our editors learned valuable lessons.

First and foremost, judging a person without understanding their history serves no purpose other than to form preconceived notions that often times are rooted in misnomers. In doing so, you may miss an opportunity to learn from those whose journey may serve as a beacon along your own road to growth. Secondly, we must accept the reality that life will be littered with obstacles and unfortunate circumstances. People we love and trust will hurt and deceive us. Employees will dis-appoint. Society will not always conform to our expectations. In order to be happy, content and successful you must learn to turn these reali-ties around and view them from the opposite end. Stop weighing your-self down by constantly reflecting on all the times life did not please you. Consider instead the day you sealed that lucrative contract, or your spouse surprised you with a thoughtful word or gesture, or your children brought home good grades. It's basically an exercise in grati-tude and the fundamental message of *"The Other 99 T. Y.M.E.S"*. This book will teach you to appreciate the good in your life (people and circumstances) and encourage you to set aside your frustrations and anger once you have looked at the bigger picture. No one situa-tion will ever be worth tarnishing the brighter outlook. Carlos Wallace will impart the importance of thinking more about the good in order to deflect the pain of the bad. To maintain a positive attitude despite the negativity that surrounds you. To appreciate circumstances that help you evolve not because you are impervious to hurt and disappoint-ment, but because you are accepting of joy. The book, much like *"Life Is Not Complicated, You Are"* is an odyssey into a part of your behavior and recesses of your psyche that you may not have fully tapped into. At the end of the journey, prepare to view life through a completely dif-ferent lens. Prepare to appreciate and value *"The Other 99 T.Y.M.E.S"*.

Liz Faublas, Anchor
Founder of Million$Pen, Ink.

BY THE GRACE of God and with eternal thanks for the support (and patience) of my dearest friends and family, I can say proudly and with a humble heart: I have finally completed my very first book, **"Life Is Not Complicated, You Are: Turning Your Biggest Disappointments Into Your Greatest Blessings".** In it, I chronicled how the principles my beloved parents and grandparents imparted helped me conquer life's challenges and, more importantly, appreciate its blessings.

Through their wisdom and guidance, I found strength, discovered insight, developed my faith and nurtured a desire to be a constant source of encouragement in the lives I touch directly and indirectly. Lessons that help us survive our greatest difficulties should be shared. I call it this dynamic a **"transfer of strength"** and had a positive rippling effect! I figured if I could help spare at least one person a night of tears, a day of hopelessness, a moment of despair and a second of sadness, then **"Life Is Not Complicated, You Are"** would be more successful than I could have ever imagined. I invite you to share your thoughts, experiences and stories of triumph. Let's do our part to create the most powerful transfer of strength the world has ever seen and begin a cycle of affirmative thinking that turns life's biggest disappointments into its greatest blessings!

"Reality Has No Filters" designed by Liz Faublas

"REALITY HAS NO FILTERS"

THERE ARE TIMES in most of our lives when tough circumstances, unexpected challenges and our deepest fears become so overwhelming we would rather run from them instead of tackling the issue head on. We convince ourselves that by turning a blind eye to the reality of the situation, it will miraculously disappear. If only it were that easy. Nothing will ever be solved if we wallow in the darkness of denial.

As someone who has dealt with his fair share of disappointment, I've learned the best way to cope with trouble is to approach every situation with eyes wide open; focused and determined. It's an innate quality that I develop every day. I discipline my mind to see past distractions, to scrutinize deceptive tendencies and to pay careful attention to details whether I am conversing with others or I'm just a passive observer. I also always do my best to consider the possible outcome(s) for any situation. I believe this vigilance is one of my greatest strengths. It allows me to remain two steps ahead of my doubters; to be acutely aware of my surroundings. Some call it a sixth sense or a "third eye". For me, it is merely the understanding that the mind is a machine that can be calibrated and the senses that feed the machine optimized for maximum potency. Clarity and peace of mind are powerful tools. Achieving either (and both) is only possible when we allow ourselves to "see" life in all its variance. The good and especially the bad. I know far too many people who prefer to shield their mind's eye from the truth. They live in a perpetual state of denial, hoping their problems will cease to exist if they pretend they are not there. However shutting out your problems does not dismiss them. Ignorance is not bliss. On the contrary, it creates an opportunity for those problems to grow. Avoidance becomes a form of self-sabotage. Your cognitive functions (with regard to the predicament you've been ignoring) virtually grind to a halt. You can't think lucidly nor can you "see" clearly. Eventually, you are blindsided (pardon the pun) by a now unmanageable dilemma you never acknowledged and therefore could not address.

The image, "**Reality Has No Filters**" is an illustration of how life should be lived. It is never prudent to bury our heads in the sand when in distress or faced with adversity; to place our hands over our eyes in a feeble attempt to hide from the inevitable. "**Reality Has No Filters**" is intended to reinforce the premise of a 20/20 approach to dealing with our problems, whatever they may be. Keep your eyes and your mind open. Don't be blinded by filters like fear, uncertainty, pessimism and negativity. Philosopher Lao Tzu wrote: *Life is a series of natural and spontaneous changes. Don't resist them - that only creates sorrow. Let reality be reality. Let things flow naturally forward in whatever way they like.*

Live life with no filters.

Carlos Wallace (age 8)

1

CROSS CHECK

THE DAY WAS picture perfect. There was not a cloud in the sky. Meteorologists described the atmosphere, the temperature, and everything about the weather as ideal: one for the record books.

An announcement to board the airplane came in a muffled, distorted alert that passengers strained to hear. Many took their cues from the stressed-out moms busily gathering diaper bags, discarded bags of chips and squirming children as they scrambled frantically to the boarding area. Others, in a less frenzied state, ambled through the maze of cell phone and laptop charger cords and stepped over carry-on bags carelessly set aside—orphaned by carriers whose faces disappeared into the white-hot glow of their cell phones, undoubtedly trying to binge on the final moments of data usage before being banished to the realm of "airplane mode."

It took longer than usual to board the airliner. The flight was completely full and the jetway was swelling with impatient ticket holders, mostly because passengers were taking an unreasonable amount of time searching for an overhead bin with enough room to store their carry-on items. Flight attendants began making the first of the announcements: "Ladies and gentlemen, if you are unable to safely store your bags in one of the overhead compartments, please return to the front of the plane. Your bags will have to be tagged and checked in. You can pick them up when we arrive at your final destination." An orchestra of sighs, moans and whispered expletives filled the cabin. This was going to be a long flight.

As the last of the passengers finally settled into their seats, travelers eager to silence the chaos and adjust to the recycled air circulating through the cabin fussed with the fans and slipped on their headsets, the official "please do not disturb" sign.

A few voyagers were visibly excited to discover the in-flight entertainment was a comedy show featuring the latest wave of stand-up comics from the acclaimed Sol-Caritas entertainment company. Artists included Cocoa Brown, Piper the Comedian, Comedian Gross'Mann, Liz Faublas, Billy Sorrells and Ken Boyd. This provided reassurance that the trip would, at the very least, be enjoyable. The flight attendants, who had been busily assisting frazzled moms, accommodating disgruntled businessmen and securing unaccompanied minors, made their way up and down the aisle to ensure everyone was complying with proper flight procedures. The captain instructed them to prepare the cabin for take-off, prompting one attendant- whose uniform was slightly faded from years of wear and her face etched with fine lines that belied her ample experience- to assume her usual position at the front of the cabin. Her much younger counterpart, clearly a novice and noticeably unsure, occupied the rear, feigning an air of confidence. Moments later, the massive plane was gliding effortlessly down the runway with enough g-force to push its inhabitants gently against the backs of their seats. A whine from a baby, a final text good-bye, a few ears popping, some uneasy passengers who have never been comfortable flying making the sign of the cross. Wheels up.

"Ladies and gentlemen, my name is Alice. On behalf of our entire flight crew, I would like to welcome you aboard Sol Airlines Flight 637, with non-stop service from Houston Hobby to New York's LaGuardia

Airport. If you had not planned on being in New York, I suggest you learn all you can about the Statue of Liberty because you are going to need to kill some time before you catch the flight you were supposed to be on (scattered laughter). You are on board a Boeing 747 under the command of Captain Charles Andrews. Captain Andrews informs us that our flying time will be approximately three hours and thirty minutes. Based on an update from the Aviation Weather Center, the captain expects we will be experiencing some in-flight turbulence shortly after we reach our 40,000 feet cruising altitude. We will do our best to keep you safe and comfortable. With that in mind, we ask that you take the safety information card out of the seat pocket in front of you and follow along as we perform our safety demonstrations." At the end of the routine presentation, the attendant flashed a rehearsed smile and added, "We appreciate your attention. On behalf of all Sol-Air employees worldwide, thank you for flying with us." Those were the last words 287 people would ever hear.

What you just read was a dramatization. A recounting of events that, for many travelers, represents a typical experience: you pack, head to the airport and board a flight fully expecting to arrive at your destination. In this particular instance, what began as an ordinary day ended in tragedy.

We've seen these headlines far too many times. On March 8, 2014, Malaysia Airlines Flight MH370 departed from Kuala Lumpur International Airport and was due to arrive in Beijing at 06:30 (22:30 GMT). According to reports, the plane lost contact less than an hour after takeoff. No distress signal or message was sent. The Malaysia Airlines plane had 239 people onboard. As of the time of this writing, the plane, crew and all passengers onboard are still missing.

The country talked about the unfortunate tragedy for months. Every day for weeks following the crash, the media discussed this missing plane. Officials searched the vast area where they believed the airliner went down for hours every single day for weeks. It was all anyone could

#WeAreSol

think about (until the next tragic occurrence). Incidents like these have instilled a sense of fear in the hearts of some travelers who believe each time they board a plane could be their last. And while no one can predict when a plane will encounter a disaster I believe we have lost sight of one critical fact: Although any time a flight crashes to earth is unquestionably a catastrophic event, keep in mind the number of flights that arrive at their destination safely. Tens of thousands a day, without incident. Too often we tend to focus on one unfortunate event without considering the countless occasions the outcome was favorable.

According to the Federal Aviation Administration (FAA), 15,461 air traffic controllers handle an average of 50,000 flights a day. Each day, 1.7 million passengers travel by plane in the U.S. safely. But you ask, what about the crashes? Well, let's take one more look at that aspect of flying and then draw a comparison that will better explain how we can find an optimistic view.

The crashes of a Germanwings A320 in March of 2015 (deliberately caused by the co-pilot, Andreas Lubitz) and a Metrojet A321 in October of 2015 (due to a suspected bomb) account for the vast majority of that year's aviation fatalities as reported in the Telegraph. According to the Aviation Safety Network (ASN), there were 14 other fatal crashes in 2015, resulting in 186 deaths for a total of 560. Take away the two deliberate crashes and it would have been the *least* deadly year for aviation since ASN's records began. When you count the number of accidents resulting in fatalities, 2015 was the safest ever year for flying.

Air traffic controllers handled 51 million flights (commercial, general aviation and military operations) in 2010. Incidents in the Middle East, India and Pakistan accounted for more than six out of 10 aviation deaths that year, as the fatal accident rate worsened from one per 1.5 million flights in 2009 - the industry's safest year - to one in every 1.3 million flights in 2010, according to Ascend Consultancy. 828 people died that year (the industry's worst in decades.)

As an added frame of reference, consider this: the same year, 32,885 people died in motor vehicle traffic crashes in the United States according to the U.S. Department of Transportation National Highway Traffic Safety Administration. While this was the lowest number of fatalities since 1949, the figure is vastly greater than the airline statistics recorded in the same period. Yet we still feel safer riding in a car than flying.

Detailing these facts in no way suggests any lack of sympathy or empathy for anyone affected by the unfathomable loss of friends, family and loved ones who perish in a plane (or a car) crash. The whole point of *"The Other 99 T.Y.M.E.S"* is to encourage all readers to retrain their way of thinking about these catastrophic events. Instead of being held hostage by the fear of what *can* go (or has gone) wrong, consider each and every time circumstances ended favorably. Yes, bad things happen. Yes, we will encounter pain and loss. We will suffer disappointment. There will be enough times in life where you will be compelled to succumb to hardship and tempted to fold in on yourself and accept gloom and doom. *"The Other 99 T.Y.M.E.S"* is written in such a way as to motivate people to say to themselves, "Things may be hard now, but I'm alive, I'm healthy, I have a job, a place to live, a loving spouse, and beautiful children! Life really does go on and I have been afforded an opportunity to go on with it." 99 encourages you to enlarge your thinking and seize the benefits that lie ahead instead of shrinking your vision to dwell on setbacks. Don't be managed by the likelihood of mishaps. Be motivated by the promise of favor!

Now is the time to realize your potential and look beyond disappointment and focus on blessings. They are all around you, if you only take the time to welcome them into your life.

I'm Carlos Wallace. Welcome to *"The Other 99 T.Y.M.E.S."*

2

SCREEN SHOT

EVER WISH YOU could capture a moment in time and forever store it in your memory? A special occasion you never want to end? Like a romantic evening you want to last forever? Or the feeling you get when you come to the end of a good book and sigh because you've identified with the story or characters so much you want to know more. How about that random text, voicemail or email that completely changes your day for the better?

It would be great to embed those moments and that feeling of contentment, euphoria or love in your mind's eye and refer back to that memory when life has you down. They would become a kind of mental "screen shot" and literally serve as the most valuable archive you could have: a permanent and positive reference point you could access whenever you need to recollect the importance of *"The Other 99 T.Y.M.E.S"* Think about it as the perfect default memory! Let me further describe the concept in terms most can relate to.

We live in a world powered by technology: cell phones, iPads, tablets, laptops and personal computers. The digital age is expanding with each new breakthrough, technological advancement and innovative app. As society's need to be informed, entertained and remain connected evolves, so too do the numerous means of satisfying these fixes. Social media could very well be the most pervasive (and persuasive) medium that exists to date! The videos, personal stories, news links that flood Facebook timelines and Twitter feeds can actually determine the course of some people's day by changing their mindset or planting a seed of thought or opinion. Former judge and current (as of this writing) President of Trinidad and Tobago, Anthony Carmona, wrote, "Social media websites are no longer performing the envisioned function of creating a positive communication link among friends, family and professionals. It is a veritable battleground, where insults fly from the human quiver, damaging lives, destroying self-esteem and harming a person's sense of self-worth." I agree. Social media can be an onerous invasion of the psyche.

Here is where you can actually benefit from this staggering surge of electronic stimuli: tap into this phalanx of texts, emails and pictures you receive every day (some that stress you out, frustrate, irritate or educate you), and hone in on the few that add meaning to your life—the two or three that make you smile, or the ten out of 100 that bring you happiness. "Screen shot" them, whether literally or figuratively. Store them in a safe place on your phone or laptop or in the recesses of your mind. And when you are blindsided by that one negative message, experience or picture…immediately access your defaults. Replay those positive images like a slideshow—all the while reminding yourself that for every one bad correspondence several positive ones prevail. Ultimately, it is about taking something you use every day and using it as a vital survival mechanism; a tool to help you maintain your sanity.

Validation was one of the most read chapters in *"Life Is Not Complicated, You Are"*. That pleases me. The premise is vitally important. The need for approval and the desire for "material things" to compensate for some void or another; the need for "trophies" and awards as a way to prove one's worth or importance; these are among the most debilitating mindsets I have ever encountered. There are few things that weigh on a person's ability to grow and thrive more than insecurity. One critique, one insult, one harsh act could cripple a person who is not confident enough in their own skin to ignore the comments. And the power social media has to frame a person's perception certainly does not help. The most liberating feeling in the world is to not give the opinions of others (good or bad) any traction.

I challenge you, the reader, to capture (screen shot) a positive image of yourself and refer back to that perspective whenever confronted with negativity and criticism or when you are tempted to resort to outside influences to build self-esteem. I want you to identify your strengths or talents and to find something about yourself that makes you unique and special and refer to that image each time you find yourself feeling insecure or unsure. Why? Because you need to arm yourself. Insecurity is a powerful enemy. It forces people to use make-up, plastic surgery, collagen injections and liposuction; to nip, tuck, throw up, push up, suck in and laser. Folks also spend money they don't have on clothes and accessories they don't need to fill a void. And no matter how much they invest in their own physical reconstruction (or in some cases deconstruction), they are still unhappy with who they see in the mirror. Don't get me wrong. We all do things to enhance our personal appearance, some more than others. But changing what's on the outside will not resolve deep-rooted issues. Whatever your God-given shell, the most extreme make over is useless if you are not even comfortable in your own skin. True beauty comes from the inside out. We have to work on our mental, emotional, spiritual and physical well-being in order to be truly happy and accept who we are. Eat right, exercise, pray, meditate, find a hobby, spend quality time with friends and family and always schedule "me" time. Confidence is by far the best armor. An image of you at your most confident is a powerful screen shot.

One year, we presented our parents with our Christmas list. My sister Shasie's number one request that holiday season was a Cabbage

Hello, Mr. Wallace. From your book, I was able to inherit many great principles. With these principles stored in my mi... along with bot... and determina... am able to obt... wise words hav... me and provided... helpful tips allow... create a life in whi... to take more contr... to thank you for ma... an impact on my life.

10:00 PM

10:44 PM

90%

Wed, 09/30/2015

I know I joke with you and give you a hard time.. However, you really make a difference with your story, journey and book. The students learn so much fro

6:00

m you and thank you so much for being a part of there lives. You have touched more people at Lonestar than you know..

16:00

68% 9:08 PM

CALL   MORE

748450

Wednesday, February 3, 2016

Los...my baby wants to know can she do her black history project about you?

Text message 8:47 PM

Patch doll. Those dolls were in high demand and very difficult to come by. They sold out quickly so if you wanted one you needed to act swiftly or risk having a very disappointed seven-year-old on your hands. And believe me when I tell you that my little sister did not like being disappointed! My mother planned way ahead. She made her way bright and early one morning to our local Wal-Mart. And this was long before the chain began doing business as Walmart (no hyphen)! She made a beeline toward the toy counter, chose her doll, got out her wallet, made a down payment and watched the clerk place the coveted Cabbage Patch doll on lay-away. Done deal. Or, so we thought.

Suffice it to say, my sister talked about that doll for months (without knowing our mother was about to make her Christmas wish come true). The day finally arrived for my mother to pick up the doll. It was a few days before Christmas. There was one fly in the ointment though. Emergency oral surgery. Yes, the night before she was due to bring the doll home my mother was in excruciating pain. She contacted her dentist who, by the grace of God, was able to schedule an appointment with an oral surgeon the next morning. My momma woke up, got ready and headed to the doctor's office where she had two of her wisdom teeth extracted. Hours later, with a bag full of painkillers, a mouth full of gauze and a wallet bearing her final payment, she was standing at the Wal-Mart counter praying the cashier would hurry up and retrieve her daughter's gift. It was not that she was so excited to pick it up (which I am sure she was). She was tired, woozy from anesthesia, irritated and wanted nothing more than to get home and go to bed. Finally, after a few minutes (during which she feared they had lost her investment) she was finally presented with the package. She, of course, checked to see that everything was in order. Upon opening the package, the evening took a decisively dramatic (and ugly) turn. My mother stood at that counter staring at a *white* Cabbage Patch doll. My mother did not pay for a white Cabbage Patch doll. She set aside a *black* one. And that was the one she was leaving the

11

Fwd: Los the wife and I had been seriously considering seperation and possible divorce. But bro after reading Legacy in your book I had no choice but to think again. Guys at work always talkin about how good your book is but now I've seen it for myself. Keep doing what you do brotha, you never know who is reading your work. Thanks again. Keep in touch.

3:01 PM

store with. A fact made known to anyone within ear shot. Through a litany of gauze muffled expletives and strongly worded declarations, my mother raised the roof off that store. Within minutes she was surrounded by managers trying to quiet her down and security guards ready to act if the situation escalated further, which by all accounts seemed inevitable. Anyone who knew Alice Wallace will attest to the fact that she did not appreciate incompetence, especially when it came to business and principles. She wanted what she paid for and was not going to leave until she got it. They offered her a discount on the doll. No deal. They offered her the option to choose another doll (white). No deal. They offered to refund her money. Definitely, no deal. After about an hour, Mrs. Alice Wallace—mouth full of bloody gauze, cheeks swollen, face red hot with frustration and a kick in her step that could only be described as pure satisfaction (with a hint of "bet you won't mess with me again" attitude)—strolled out of that store, black Cabbage Patch doll in hand.

That was my momma.

The images from that day as my mother described them will forever be imprinted on my brain. I did not realize how entertaining the story was (once you got past the drama and seriousness of the actual incident) until I recounted it to my creative consultant. She immediately suggested (well, she literally insisted through bursts of teary laughter) that I include the story in this book. Admittedly, I was puzzled at first about why (and how) she felt the incident fit with the format of *"The Other 99 T.Y.M.E.S"* However, after we replayed the events and talked about this particular chapter and its intended message, the light went on.

I could interpret that memory in two ways.

First: View my mother as an irrational, angry black woman whose dislike for the "white doll" spoke to a general deep-seated hatred for white people. And by behaving so erratically when presented with the toy, she was setting a dangerous precedent by teaching her own children that it was OK to hate white people. So much so that anything that even smacks of that culture is forbidden to cross the threshold of our home. Even a white Cabbage Patch doll.

Or, I could construe the events of that evening as I know to be more accurate. My mother spent a year diligently paying for a doll that her only daughter desired. She chose the doll she wanted at the beginning of the year and fully expected to receive it when she made her final payment. She held up her end of the deal. Moreover, my mother wanted that doll because it was a reflection of her baby girl; the doll her daughter could identify with. It was not about hating the white doll. It was about loving what the black doll represented: her child, her culture. When I refer to the screen shot of that moment, I use it as a reference for what it means to love oneself: to be proud of who you are and to choose things in life that emulate that person.

The incident occurred more than three decades ago yet its implications still resonate to this day. With the tension of race relations throughout the country pulled dangerously taut and young men and women struggling to find (and protect) their identity without being divisive or confrontational, it is critical to have images we can relate to. And when we have that image we need to hold fast to it.

Now, not *all* memories deserve to be a screen shot. As with any important life decision, you should always take a step back, breathe, reflect, discern and parse out which moments are worthy of the des-ignation **"The Other 99 T.Y.M.E.S"**. Sometimes though, people cycle through countless unfavorable circumstances only to eventually de-cide the one thing that could help, the single positive alternative to living with the challenges and negative influences, is not in their best interest.

❤ 💬 ↱   ⋮

❤ [_____]

[_____] Had an amazing speaker today in #Philosophy @mrcarloswallace "The common denominator in all your problems, is yourself" -Carlos Wallace

Such was the case with Alonzo Spellman, whose difficulties I write about in the **Bittersweet** chapter. He made the choice he felt was in his best interest, whether people agreed with his decision or not. His memories (the ones that reminded him that he was a great, powerful football player), were more important; too important to wipe clean with a battery of drugs that would have silenced his demons, but simultaneously dull his prowess and take the edge off his power. Writing about Spellman was especially difficult in a book where I explore the advantages of focusing on the 99 good things; the 99 acts of kindness; the 99 times life and the people in it are benevolent to you. However, I understand that sometimes (for some people) that *one* instance is all there is, good or bad.

Many of us wage this ongoing internal war with our past. Our brains are constantly churning out scenarios we would have liked to play out, thoughts we wish we verbalized, actions we wish we'd taken. We spend way too much time thinking about what we should have, could have or would have said and done. We have entire con-versations inside our head with a ghost. Most times, the person (or people) you are burning all this energy on are not paying you any mind. They've moved on. So should you. Never spend more time worrying about somebody or some situation (that plays no significant role in your life) more than you do about yourself. In this case, you are your **Other 99 T.Y.M.E.S**! The people who care about you are your **Other 99 T.Y.M.E.S**. Why expend valuable time on would have, should have, could have, when you actually do have all the important things (and people) in your life now? Your present, your today is your screen shot.

(tl) Carlos Wallace, (bc) Aurelia Wallace),
Mom, ® Step Wallace

3

REALITY CHECK

WHEN I WAS in the Navy I travelled the globe. I encountered several cultures and lifestyles and soon came to the realization that an entire world existed beyond Jacksonville, Texas. This was common among military men and women. We obviously faced everyday challenges, performed specific duties and, invariably, became better for it. The seriousness of being part of Operation Desert Storm-the first major foreign crisis for the United States after the end of the Cold War- was never lost upon us. The Gulf War became a lesson in history and thrust us into the history books. But in the midst of combat, we learned a great deal about mankind and its many different races, creeds and beliefs. From week to week, we were literally thrust into a whole new world! It was definitely a mind-blowing experience and culture shock for this good ol' country boy from East Texas. But, you take in every detail of your environment and you adapt. Those of us who were open-minded evolved.

I never realized how differently others talked, thought and lived in the "big city." I met men and women from Chicago, New York, Dallas and even Houston that discussed issues which (up until the day I enlisted) were foreign to me. The greatest of these topics was the prevailing culture of racial inequality. I can say with all honesty that, for the most part, I grew up in a tight-knit community and the degree of bigotry my East Coast comrades described did not resonate with me despite a couple of personal encounters that revealed there were, shall we say, "differences" between the races. I discussed a couple of these experiences in **"Life Is Not Complicated, You Are"**. I also note a few conflicts in this book. Still, I took it all in if, for no other reason, to broaden my proverbial horizons. But no matter how worldly I became, there was always that one part of me that never forgot where I came from and how simple life was there. For many of us, staring down the reality of war, far from home, asleep among strangers, that familiarity and those memories and ties kept us going. They gave us a reason to persevere and toughened us up. Yet, no matter how much I learned from my experiences, nothing could have prepared me for one of the most life-altering moments of my life.

When I was honorably discharged from the U.S. Navy and returned to my hometown of Jacksonville, I discovered some of the constants I clung to my whole life had shifted. It was not some dramatic, obvious transformation that settled in as soon as I re-entered the city limits. It was slow. Subtle. Unexpected. But when I came face-to-face with the conversion, the ensuing reality check hit me like a runaway freight train. The damage it caused shattered my perception of friendship, made me re-evaluate the concepts of loyalty and integrity, and nearly ruined my life.

By all accounts it was a normal evening in our small town, at least by Jacksonville standards. I met up with one of my friends since kindergarten. I had of course been away in the Navy and him in the Army. He was stationed in Europe and I was in Japan. After being away for so long we had some catching up to do. We were riding around, talking and joking and sharing stories. He had been going on and on about this girl who he was smitten with. To hear him describe this young woman you would think she hung the moon. We arrived at her house and she jumped in the truck, excited and full of conversation. I wish I could say there was a hint of uncertainty in

Carlos Wallace (age 18)
San Diego, California

the air; some indication that something terribly wrong was about to unfold. However, there was nothing; not even a gut instinct. We were busy laughing and chatting. After some time, the young lady needed to use the restroom so we pulled into a neighborhood gas station. None of us thought twice about the two people who were engaged in a heated dispute at the only other pump station. However, as the minutes ticked off and the argument got more intense all I could think of was, it's only a couple of weeks before Christmas and this drama was just not necessary—a sentiment that I shared with the pair in the hopes it would diffuse their argument. Granted, I was interfering in a situation that was none of my concern. But I had just witnessed more unrest, death and war than I wanted to remember during Desert Storm. Tonight, I was more interested in keeping the peace. I am not sure what it was that set one of the men off but it did not take much for me to realize my jovial holiday spirit was not welcome. Whatever the reason, he unleashed a racial assault so brutal we were all stunned. I heard his words echo in my brain with such force it rattled my consciousness. Nothing could have prepared me for that one epithet my Navy buddies warned me about. It was guttural and fierce and it was ringing through the air. All this in the town which, up until that moment, I believed was different than the big cities. There it was, the word that reminded me hate is everywhere: "Fuck you, nigger." My mind raced. Several less than seasonally appropriate words were exchanged. There was nothing merry about the messy discourse that ensued.

Call it military training, a judgment call or just plain disbelief that our night had taken such a turn, but my better judgment prevailed. When I realized there was no pacifying this man I backed off and got back in the vehicle. I knew this could only get worse and I did not want to get caught up in any drama. Before I could think he was at my car door trying to force his way inside. Instinctively, I used the door to create a barrier between us, but he was close enough for me to smell the alcohol on his breath. I'm not sure if it was the threat of physical violence or the lingering impact of the term he just used that unnerved me the most; however, at that moment I lost all sense of reason. Only one recourse made sense. I reached under the seat, grabbed the licensed firearm that was sitting in the hollow well of the floorboard and in one swift motion struck him with the butt of the gun. Stunned, he reared back and stumbled to the ground. The arctic chill in the air was unforgiving. As soon as I struck the man, the cold blast caused my hand to seize up and I dropped the gun. My immediate concern was that the man I had just pistol whipped could take hold of that weapon and exact revenge. I scrambled to retrieve the firearm. At the same time, my buddy exited the vehicle brandishing his own piece. In plain sight mind you. And clear enough for the gas station attendant to take note and report the escalating incident to the local officials.

The concept of time eluded me. It seemed as if it took mere minutes for the Jacksonville Police to arrive at the scene. Upon arrival the officer, who I happened to know, asked me if I had a weapon. I admitted I did. He asked why I struck the man. I replied I was in fear for my life. My estimate of time and memory of the events that had just transpired were ambiguous given the traumatic nature of the conflict. However, I was taken into custody. As the officer tightened the heavy metal handcuffs around my wrist I looked down at the man whose rage had precipitated my actions and realized I had just screwed up. Badly. During the ride to the county holding cell, the police officer gave me one of the most critical lectures of my life. He essentially tried to make sense of why a young man who had just been honorably discharged from the Navy and had just taken a job with one of the most prestigious railroad companies in the country would risk throwing his life away over a word. A name. The racist ramblings of someone with nothing to lose. It was not my finest hour. Nor was this some miraculous "Aha" moment. His words were not resonating with me. How could he not understand how violated I felt? I was just called one of the most hateful names in our country's history! And here he was, chastising me? Really? My mind was spinning. I had so many questions. How did I get here? What will my parents say? What will Granddaddy say? I would find out soon enough.

The ride home with my mother, who had come to bail me, was a reality check of epic proportions. I likened it to a medieval form of torture. We actually spoke to the judge that very day and he also asked me what my mother and the police officer had already asked: why on earth would I risk throwing my life away for someone who, at that moment, was home and carefree while I faced as much as twenty years in prison for aggravated assault? Now it was starting to sink in.

I sat alongside my mom humiliated, chastened and dejected. Momma was neither compassionate nor forgiving. She let me know in no uncertain terms that I was to leave our home in Jacksonville and go back to Houston immediately. She was disgusted by my behavior. The language she used I cannot repeat. Her harsh response hurt more than any foul word some stranger I would likely never see again called me. I had disappointed my mother, my grandparents and myself for nothing substantial enough to warrant any of this angst.

Because I had no record and my family's reputation preceded the circumstances, my case progressed swiftly. As if the incident and the repercussions were not enough to redefine my view of the world, days after I was exonerated for acting in self-defense, it was brought to my attention that the "good friend" I had been riding with, when questioned about the events leading up to the episode, told officials that I not only "planned" to engage in an altercation that night, I declared specifically that I was on a mission. He said I was targeting a "white man." Those were "Benedict's" exact words.

Were it not for my clean record, my military background and my standing in the community (and that of my family), "Benedict's" statement might have seemed credible. However, the report was

23

Carlos Wallace (age 19)
Sasebo, Japan

® *Carlos Wallace, (l) Lorenza McCullough*
Broadway Comedy Club 2016 (New York City)

eventually discredited. But not before this warning from one of the officers in charge of the case (a man who just happened to know my family): "Carlos, in this world you will come to discover not everyone who says he/she is your friend is really a friend". Some of the most difficult lessons learned in one's lifetime are revealed when least expected. Reality hit home!

For months I carried a serious chip on my shoulder. My defenses were high, trust was low and my skepticism was in overdrive while my anger at times misplaced. Slowly though, rational thinking began to prevail. I also started to realize my story was not unique. Most of us have that one friend we thought would never turn on us. I discovered the word "friend" is a label anyone can try on. You decide who is best suited to wear it. Choose wisely. The most dangerous among us come dressed as angels and we learn too late they are the devil in disguise. What a harsh truth. But this was by *no means* the greatest epiphany to materialize from the experience. In my disappointment, I almost lost sight of the fact that Benedict was the exception in my life and not the rule. I had been focusing so much on one person who turned against me, all the while ignoring the group of friends who had (and have) always had my back and would never dream of betraying me. Friends who no matter what stand with me. Through the death of my grandparents and parents, my divorce, my most difficult moods— even while I built a business from the ground up—these friends never abandoned me. Like brothers, they love me. And ultimately, that is all that matters. Jon Jon, Vinson, Lorenza, Cody are the prime examples of *"**The Other 99 T.Y.M.E.S**".* When it comes to true, unconditional friendship, it's the good that should be the focus.

An argument. A minor disagreement. A major feud. If you have been close friends with anyone for a significant period of time you've been through some of these skirmishes, to varying degrees and probably more than once. These are simply circumstances that test the bonds of any friendship, no matter how close you are. Depending

26

on the strength of the relationship, level of communication and one's tolerance for discord, many people are able to get past normal skirmishes unscathed. You hash it out, resolve the issue and move forward. You certainly do not let one squabble derail a friendship. Some, however, do just that. Far too often, good friends bump heads and the ensuing rift drives a wedge between them without considering:

- How close they are
- How much they appreciate one another
- How much they sacrifice for each other

They allow one meltdown to:

- Wipe memories clean
- Void all good deeds
- Break down an alliance that took years to build

In the heat of the moment, rational thinking tends to elude us (as evidenced by the story I shared in the beginning of this chapter). Why is this the case? Let's ponder this query.

Why, despite all the times you praised your friend for a job well done or thanked him or her for helping you or shared personal thoughts— knowing this person was one of the few who "get" you- are all those moments eclipsed by one misstep? If we all stopped for a moment (mid-grudge), took a step back following our spats and considered these simple questions, I assure you there would be more reconciliation among friends. Granted, some flare ups push a friendship to the point of no return. That is just a reality. Everyone has a breaking point. You cannot fault a person that has been pushed and tested for so long for eventually pushing back. When that happens, the person reacting should not automatically be perceived as the bad one. Most people do not "all of a sudden" become mean or confrontational. They are just human and, as many of us have, reach a moment where enough is enough. Testing the wrong person can prove a massive failure for the antagonist. Give respect to get respect. You can only be Gandhi for so long before you eventually transform to Malcolm X. I want to celebrate those friendships that have withstood the test of time. Those bonds that are tightly woven by threads of experience, loyalty and commitment. When you realize how rare and valuable those alliances are, only then will you fully comprehend why one conflict should never outweigh *"The Other 99 T.Y.M.E.S"* Harmony can prevail.

You may believe, in order to apply the concept of *"The Other 99 T.Y.M.E.S"* in your friendships that you have to bend too far, compromise too much, or conform unequivocally to others. That's not true, but one should always make an effort to find a middle ground. That *gray area* is where compromise exists. Admittedly, this "median territory" is not one I came to inhabit easily. As far as I was concerned (and for as long as I can remember) my views on life have been strictly black and white. I firmly believed that this perplexing grey area is where misunderstanding resided. It was that aspect of any discussion, debate, argument or ordinary conversation that left the door wide open to each person's individual interpretation of facts, events and recollection and that often led to confusion (and further disagreement). I disliked the term and what it embodied my entire adult life. Today, as much as it surprises even me to admit it, I not only advocate for the gray, I *am* the gray. My understanding of the concept came with maturity and growth. I learned through a series of trial and error that the median space is actually what's missing in our daily walk.

We live in a world with an ever-growing population. Personal space these days is at a premium. Physically, we are practically tripping over our fellow man. Mentally and spiritually, the divide among us seems to widen. Everyone has their own opinions about life-altering circumstances that affect society daily. Religion, education, and of course—as I write this during the most contentious and talked about Presidential campaign season in generations—politics. It's fine to stand firm on our individual beliefs. Doing so without consideration for opposing views is where problems lie. We live in a society where people feel they have to be right, no matter what. If we subscribe to that narrow view, the critical gray area is compromised.

Don't get me wrong, my principles will always be hardcore and so should yours. The foundation that my parents and grandparents instilled in me is unyielding, especially the principle that teaches me to keep God first in all I do. But a firm stance on the tenets I hold dear should not preclude my trying to understand where others are coming from and where they may be trying to go.

As an organizer I learned that this approach is the key to success in all campaigns. A negotiator has to consider the needs and demands of all parties in order to find common ground, and ultimately, find solutions. In a relationship, prudent application of the gray theory is a key ingredient in assuring years of happiness: "'til death do us part." Balance is at the center of success, satisfaction and a lifetime of love.

The gray breaks down barriers. When I was in the Navy, everyone fell under the purview of "navy gray." It is the military's way of reminding its enlisted personnel that they are all equal. Man or woman, black or white, young or old, everyone was navy gray. With God's grace I can proudly say a better understanding of this concept has helped me ameliorate disputes, mend fences that appeared hopeless, and find light in the midst of darkness.

The flip side of this is, we must realize that people do not *have* to conform to one another. We are, after all, ultimately beholden only to ourselves. Now, the people who care (and matter) will respect you for who you are and conduct themselves accordingly; compromising when necessary because you are worth it.

As Sophocles taught, "Kindness is ever the begetter of kindness."

4

DOOR MONEY

IF I HAD to pinpoint a single characteristic that most people I've encountered in my adult life possess, it is the tendency to focus far too much attention on insignificant circumstances; an inclination to reflect expressly on the inconsequential. Quite simply, they rack their brains about the wrong things. It's a trait that keeps them from making significant, substantive strides in their lives because priorities become blurred and the bigger picture is overlooked. The **Other 99 T.Y.M.E.S** are forgotten. Trust me, I can relate. I've been a victim of this state of mind. In fact, had I given in to the distraction on one occasion I would have missed the opportunity of a lifetime. I call this phenomenon focusing on "door money." It's a phrase I coined when I began producing comedy shows throughout the country. To focus on door money means one is paying so much attention to the amount of money they are making at the door they do not consider there is much more profit to be made inside a venue. The real investment, the hard work and potential for success, begin after you cross the threshold. People who are distracted by door money, neglect the production and the audi-ence. Money becomes their god. They sacrifice their reputation in favor of building revenue. Believe me, the former is more difficult to recover if lost.

When my first book was published, my editor and publicist at Million$Pen, Ink. kept me pretty busy. As I mentioned in an earlier chapter, MDPI booked several radio and television interviews throughout the country. The message in *"Life Is Not Complicated"* was resonating with audiences I had not even dreamed would consider reading it, much less be interested in talking with me about its subject matter. Of course, I did not complain. After all, this is the kind of attention any new author welcomes. Even if it meant constantly being on the go and travelling for days at a time. There came a time when my life was no longer my own. If a network called I was packed and ready to go. If an organization or school wanted to book me as a keynote speaker, I obliged no questions asked. The rush was exhilarating and exhausting at the same time. We would schedule speaking engagements weeks in advance. At the time these events were booked, everything seemed great...in theory!

On one particular morning I awoke at the crack of dawn to make my way to my third speaking engagement that week. I'd slept maybe four hours. The venue was a local Houston school and the Director was very excited I was finally available to speak with the students, faculty and staff. I was honored and humbled by the opportunity. Still, I was beyond tired. To say I was dreading getting out of my bed (on a bleak, rainy, cold morning) would be an understatement. I sparred with the snooze button for 20 minutes and pleaded with the pillows to smother me with a few more seconds of sleep. I lost both bouts by unanimous decision. I showered, dressed, scarfed down a quick breakfast and got into my truck all the while dreading the day ahead. I called my publicist to ask if this was absolutely necessary. The rain was relentless, the fog created dangerous driving conditions and the traffic made me want to bite through the steering wheel. She replied, emphatically and with no mercy, "Yes, so suck it up and make sure you are on time!" I could not remember the last time I was so dispas-sionate about attending an event. To add insult to injury what should have been a 20-minute trip turned into a one-hour ordeal because of traffic. I arrived at the school on time but extremely irritated. Were it not for the warm reception I received upon entering the building, I am not sure I would have had the disposition to fulfill my obligation. However, the pleasant atmosphere encouraged me. When I caught a glimpse of the eager faces that had gathered to hear me speak I realized I needed to shake off my annoyance and give these attendees what they deserved: an enthusiastic, positive, motivational speech about the lessons that had given me the will to make it this far in life. Basically, I needed to practice what I was preaching.

By the end of my presentation, the frustration I had been feeling completely dissipated. I was in my glory. After all, this is what it was all about! I wrote the book as a source of encouragement. I am telling the story of my life so that when anyone was faced with negativity like the kind I battled that morning, they had a source of motivation, a purpose, and a reason to persevere past the angst and frustration in order to embrace the opportunities that await. Had my day ended there, I would have been satisfied (albeit, a bit disappointed in myself for allowing my emotions to affect my work ethic and my mood.) I mingled a bit with other speakers following my presentation. It was great to talk with educators and students about the book and hear their feedback. As I continued to network, one woman took note of the book's cover and recognized me as the author. She asked if she could skim through it and of course I obliged. A few minutes later, she asked if she could have a copy. I had no idea who this woman was, but that did not matter. Once again, I obliged. You may be asking yourself, "What's the big deal? So, you gave her a book. And?" What's important to understand is, when you are an independent author marketing and promoting your life's work, giving a book away is not some arbitrary decision. A great deal of work (and cost) goes into publishing a book. While I can never put an actual price tag on the effort and the meaning behind *"Life Is Not Complicated, You Are",* I can assure you, I do not just hand over the sum of my blood, sweat and tears on a whim. However, I am also not a pretentious man. I could have been absolutely offended that she asked for a free copy of the book and insisted she either pay for it or forget about it. At that moment, it could have been all about the money and less about the fact she was obviously so intrigued by what she had read that she wanted to know more. For me, it was a no brainer.

I left the event in good spirits. I did not have much time to reflect on the experience because I had to catch a flight to New York. And then, days later, I received a phone call. It turns out, the woman I presented the book to was a professor at a local college. As we spoke about my work, I discovered we shared many of the same principles, philosophies and views on life. There was an academic connection and mutual understanding. She informed me that after reading *"Life Is Not Complicated, You Are"*, she wanted to make it available to her students. It took me a moment to realize what she was proposing. This lady (who I would come to learn is Doctor Cherry H. Sawyerr, Associate Faculty of Psychology at Lone Star College) wanted to incorporate my book, my first effort, into her academic curriculum as required reading. Within months, we received the nod from school officials. *"Life Is Not Complicated, You Are"* would be assimilated into her program. The book was met with extremely positive critiques. Students praised the message as groundbreaking, heartwarming, inspiring and life-saving. I was also invited by the Psychology Department to teach a course about the book at the college. Today, as an Adjunct Professor, I am able to instruct students (and share with faculty) about the book's integral, life-affirming message first hand.

Now that I have recounted this experience, from the rough start of my day to the fortuitous outcome, I will remind you of the point of this story. I gave that book away. I did not focus on the money I would lose by presenting this woman with the gift. I did not dwell on whether she would read the book or be impressed by my story. I did not contemplate what she could or would do for me. Remember, I had no idea she was a professor. Nor did I, in my wildest imagination,

even consider she could propel this book into the realm of academia! It was one item. One opportunity. One moment in my life. And that one act has earned me another 99 opportunities that changed the course of my future, forever. Dozens of days, experiences and encounters have set me on a path I never dreamed possible. Imagine the outcome had I been so concentrated on making money that the idea of giving away a book was not even an option? Imagine, if I had been focusing on "door money"?

Dwight D. Eisenhower once said, "I have two kinds of problems, the urgent and the important. The urgent are not important and the important are never urgent." Eisenhower is credited with creating the "Eisenhower Decision Principle" which asserts that tasks are evaluated using the criteria "important/unimportant" and "urgent/not urgent," and then placed in quadrants as part of an Eisenhower Matrix (also known as an "Eisenhower Box" or "Eisenhower Decision Matrix"), accordingly. Tasks are then handled as follows:

> ➢ *Important/Urgent quadrant are done immediately and personally (e.g. crises, deadlines, problems).*

> ➢ *Important/Not Urgent quadrant get an end date and are done personally (e.g. relationships, planning and recreation).*

> ➢ *Unimportant/Urgent quadrant are delegated (e.g. interruptions, meetings, activities).*

> ➢ *Unimportant/Not Urgent quadrant are dropped (e.g. time wasters, pleasant activities, and trivia).*

Ultimately, it's about determining what matters most to you, what's important, and what it will take to achieve your intended goal. And once you've identified these key components to growth, it's about shedding the excess, doing away with the unnecessary, and finding the value in **"The Other 99 T.Y.M.E.S"**

Jay Z, in my opinion, is one of the most prolific hip hop artists of his time. His business acumen has proven time and time again to be honed, strategic, and at times daring. Just about everything Jay Z touches turns to gold. And not by some arbitrary stroke of luck. The man does not make a move that has not been studied. Nor does he speak without purpose. It's an admirable quality because it aligns with one of my greatest philosophies: there will never be a point in anyone's life where it is acceptable to waste time. Ever. Every thought, every action, every statement should have meaning. There should always be an end game or else all you are doing is practicing for an opportunity that might never come.

During a 2013 interview on "The Breakfast Club," a nationally syndicated radio program, Jay Z was asked about the tremendous success of his music download deal with Samsung. Fans were prepared to download his highly anticipated upcoming album "Magna Carta Holy Grail" at an appointed time. You must understand, this was a BIG deal. This had never been attempted. To say that anticipation was high is an understatement. But at the appointed time, the app encountered major glitches. The program was literally overloaded with hits and shut down. Radio personality Angela Yee noted that this dilemma (to have so many hits that an app would just about short circuit) must have been a good problem. I understood what she was saying. It's a very common perception when the focus is profit or the potential for profit—when the focus is "door money." More is better, no matter the consequence. In this case, the consequence was the fact that millions of people who had been anticipating this moment, this historical event, were disappointed and frustrated. Jay Z explained that it was more important for the fans to have the experience. He related it to someone who had done everything he/she were supposed to do (buy the phone, request the app, tune in at the appointed time) only to be let down. The multi-million dollar deal was not his focus at the time. He didn't shrug his shoulders and say, "Oh well, I've got my money, screw the fans." He was more concerned with making it right and delivering what he and Samsung had promised. His reputation, his word, his credibility, his fans were more important than "door money." That story, in my mind, could not sum up this chapter any better.

Start here: each day, wake up with a plan. Don't just approach your days in an unfocused void. That state of mind leaves too much room for discontent, opposition, unhappiness and hopelessness. Small or elaborate, set a goal. Check something off your "to do" list or add something to your bucket list. Assign a deadline to your biggest objectives and stick to it so they don't become just another litany of "what ifs" and sad regrets. Occupy your thoughts with purpose and you will be so busy pursuing a meaningful future there will be no time for doubt, chaos and disappointment. Always remember the end game. Set your sights on the goal line, and not ticket sales or how much merchandise you are moving or how much profit the other team is generating. That's all "door money." Is that all you want from life? A big payday? If the answer to that is no, you understand there is more to success than the bottom line. Of course, it goes without saying that whatever you do should be rewarding. What I am stressing is, make that reward count for something more than a fat bank account. Make a difference, change the game for the better, leave a legacy, be a guide that someone else can follow and make better, and then someone else will follow that and make that better. Be the start of something that is good, revolutionary and powerful. Everything after that is a bonus!

Most times it's just about taking a step back and determining what really matters. Deliberately determine responses to the following three questions (I advise writing them down.): 1. What do I want? 2. Why do I want it? 3. How am I going to make it happen? Then tune everything and everyone else out. You do not need anyone to cosign your every decision. We think too much about things that require faith! Just be still. If we calm the mind, we would realize everything we "pray" for is already present within us! One truth that has helped me accept some of the most difficult moments and heartbreaking decisions in my life is that I already have all for which I ask. I am blessed! I am delivered from my worries! I am healed! I understand (finally) that God does not REACT to prayers or petitions. He has ACTED. It is already done. Establish the type of relationship with God that enables you to "see" this. He will light the path. That is faith. Is this easy? Not one bit. Am I overflowing with this enlightenment every minute of every day? Not at all. Do I ask why? Yes. And then, I remind myself (force myself to remember actually) that if I question, I do not believe. Eventually I fall back on the faith that calms me. It's work. I mean, you literally have to re-train your mind, heart and soul to think more in alignment with peace and reject those thoughts that unsettle you. It's a process. And you need to want it bad enough—to practice it every day until it becomes second nature. That is where I am. I'm practicing. I'm a work in progress. My incentive? Making a peaceful spirit second nature. And that is so worth the effort.

Door money. It's a distraction. It impedes judgment. It blurs focus. Chasing the almighty dollar can become the root of all evil, the bane of one's existence. We must learn to choose between lining our bank accounts and being accountable for our future. Sometimes it's not about making a ton of money in one night, only to spend the rest of your life waiting on the next payday. You will fare better planning your next move, investing time and engaging in strategic thinking in order to secure a stable, fruitful future. Which is more important to you? Instant gratification or long-term fulfillment? The choice is yours. Set your priorities accordingly.

5

GOLDEN GOOSE

I AM OFTEN asked how I choose the chapter titles for my books. I wish I could offer a profound, scintillating scenario about how vivid themes come to me unexpectedly during deep moments of reflection or following some profound, impactful experience. However, it's not that complicated. Very little about my life is. Which is why, when it comes to assigning a name to (and writing) each chapter, it is much simpler to tap directly into my life and my thoughts; to recall my daily exchanges and routines and apply those experiences to my books. For instance, my conversations with business associates, friends and family are typically so engaging that insightful ideas and concepts emerge from ordinary, everyday discussions. With regard to this chapter, I was speaking with a friend during a lunch meeting and I was sharing my assessment of a situation involving a close friend (one that I will expound on in a moment). I used the analogy of the goose that laid the golden eggs. The baffled look on his face conveyed the obvious. He did not grasp how a children's fable could possibly be used to explain the intricacies of a real life event. When I finished clarifying how the metaphor related to the issue at hand, he had no choice but to nod and agree that the comparison was perfect. For those who are not familiar with the fairytale (or who may not recall the details), here it is in a nutshell.

There was once a young farmer who inherited land from his father. The farmer was lazy and hated to work. He simply felt he was too good to perform menial tasks. So, instead of tending the land he began selling off all of the farming equipment. After all, he didn't use it anyway. Suffice it to say, it did not take long for him to run out of machinery to peddle. Eventually his source of income dried up. One day, while looking for provisions to put on the market, the farmer happened upon the chicken coop where he discovered an odd looking goose. When he lifted the bird from its nest, he found an egg that was bright yellow and glittered in the light. His first inclination was to throw it away. Surely someone was playing a trick on him. Or perhaps the egg was defective. After giving it some thought he took the egg home and, to his delight, found out it was made of pure gold. The following day he went back to the nest, lifted the goose and found another glittering, golden egg. This scenario played out for days. The farmer's prayers had been answered. He found a way to fulfill his dreams of being wealthier and more powerful than his father without breaking a sweat. The farmer soon amassed extraordinary riches, but he became greedy and impatient. Waiting for the goose to lay these eggs each day was taking too long. How ideal would it be to collect all the eggs inside the goose at one time? So, he killed the bird and cut it open only to find nothing in its belly. Much to his dismay, he soon realized that killing the goose meant there would no more golden eggs. Essentially, as a result of his avarice and hubris, he destroyed the source of his benefits. The moral of the story? In the words of Oprah Winfrey, "Be thankful for what you have and you'll end up having more. If you concentrate on what you don't have, you will never, ever have enough."

This lesson can be applied to many real-life situations. Once you have completed this chapter, you will likely find yourself comparing some of your experiences to the story. In the pages ahead we will focus on patience, loyalty, intelligence, greed, dissatisfaction and pride.

Throughout our lives we will meet individuals who benefit from the assistance of others yet are resentful of another person's goodwill. They are too proud to be an associate, an assistant or a vice president, not because they have worked hard enough to be promoted to a higher position but because they believe they are *entitled* to a greater calling. These characters consider themselves bigger than the corporation, better than the relationship or more important than the team. That way of thinking is seriously flawed. I have come to learn that under no circumstance is any proverbial player ever more significant than the collective. One scene is never more important than the bigger picture. When you switch your focus from the "we" to the "me," or the goal from "team" to "self," you upset the balance of the whole. Consequently, that selfish redistribution of effort impedes success. The tide seldom shifts in favor of a self-centered individual. When you sever ties with the unit purely for self-serving intentions, you are likely to find yourself stranded and struggling to survive; fighting to keep your head above water. What's more, there is no one to save you because you've turned your back on your comrades and snubbed your support system. What a tragedy, to stand in the middle of your world, watching everything around you fall apart, and realize that your actions precipitated this free fall! Take more time to consider the consequences of your thoughts and actions. One day, you will call out for help. Don't let bad judgment disconnect your lifelines.

I often speak candidly about my mentor, Michael L. Herzik. He is actually more than a mentor. He is the closest person I have to a dad since Aaron Lee Wallace, Jr. (a.k.a. Bigfoot) went on to glory. I admire Michael for all he has accomplished and love him for all he contributes to the lives of those around him. He is ready to help anyone in need of assistance. He is one of the most selfless people I have ever met. And most importantly, he never allows his success to dictate his behavior or determine how he treats people. Sadly, the same cannot be said for some of the people with whom he has done business (or helped at one time or another).

As a businessman, entrepreneur and attorney with decades of experience and a considerable network of associates and personal connections, Michael wields considerable influence. I describe him as a "one phone call" kind of guy because, with the swipe of his smartphone, he can change the course of a person's life or pull someone out of a bind by attaining something that was nearly impossible to come by without asking for a thing in return except the individual's gratitude. Yet far too often, men and women afforded an opportunity to excel thanks to his benevolence, dislike Michael because they would much rather be the one who has the power. What's even more disheartening to me is that many of these individuals fail to consider that he has worked many years, faced his share of obstacles, reinvented himself more than once and traversed his share of peaks and valleys to arrive at his present state of success. He earned the power. These people, like the farmer who believed so strongly that he was better than his father and did not have to work as hard to amass the same amount of success, undermine and deceive, speak ill of and do everything in their power to prove they are not only better than he is, but they also deserve more than he has. I have known this man my entire adult life and can say with 100 percent certainty that all who have applied these tactics, have met with an undesirable outcome. Not because he countered their efforts to sabotage him with some biblical, vindictive "eye for an eye" rationale. Instead, it is as described in Aesop's fable of the goose that laid the golden eggs; if one does not value the source of their benefits, they are destined to lose it. When egotistical intentions compel you to undermine someone's magnanimity, you set a series of events in motion that will lead to your demise. You break trust. You burn bridges. You jeopardize your reputation. More importantly, you ignore the 99 things that will help you for one shot at glory that proves to be unremarkable, unnecessary and unsuccessful. Nothing good arises from your actions and you definitely do not acquire the power you so desperately covet.

Carlos Wallace with mentor Michael Herzik

Robert Greene wrote in his book **48 Laws of Power**, "Always make those above you feel comfortably superior. In your desire to please or impress them, do not go too far in displaying your talents or you might accomplish the opposite – inspire fear and insecurity. Make your masters appear more brilliant than they are and you will attain the heights of power." To be honest, the theory, as written in **48 Laws,** is extreme in my opinion, although I suspect it is not to be interpreted literally. I do however agree with the general premise. To give respect where it is due is not a sign of weakness. To pay deference to pioneers or leaders is simply acknowledging that you appreciate the opportunities they provide, the jobs they make available, and the doors they open.

In 2014, Bill Gates stepped down as chairman of Microsoft. Forty years after Gates and Paul Allen founded Microsoft, Gates marked the anniversary with an email to Microsoft employees.

"Early on, Paul Allen and I set the goal of a computer on every desk and in every home. It was a bold idea and a lot of people thought we were out of our minds to imagine it was possible," Gates wrote. *"It is amazing to think about how far computing has come since then, and we can all be proud of the role Microsoft played in that revolution."*

"I hope you will think about what you can do to make the power of technology accessible to everyone, to connect people to each other, and make personal computing available everywhere. We have accomplished a lot together during our first 40 years and empowered countless businesses and people to realize their full potential. But what matters most now is what we do next. Thank you for helping make Microsoft a fantastic company now and for decades to come."

In this email, one of the most powerful, brilliant men in the history of technology—a trailblazer, a leader whose vision became the "language" 90 percent of the world uses to communicate—praises the "all" for the success of his business, giving the credit to the team and the entire company. And these were men and women who were given the opportunity to change the world, and embraced it. They were employees who chose to weather the storm instead of abandoning ship and for that they were rewarded. This is what happens when you play a role in the evolution of society. You become part of greatness. According to a *CNN Money* article, today Gates is worth nearly $80 billion, making him the world's richest man. He has also become a major figure in philanthropy. I'm sure his employees agree, it was worth being loyal and sticking it out!

Relationships (business or friendship) should never be completely about what the other person can do for you. Ask yourself: "What do I contribute? What do I bring to the table? What do I do solely for the benefit of the other person?" Not because you are going to get something out of it but because you care as much about their needs and well-being as they do yours. The irony is if you can be selfless with the right people, you are still rewarded! If you build your team up, they become stronger. Support them and they can walk more steadily. Appreciate them and who they are apart from you and they know they are respected. Uplift, encourage and honor them and they will know they are valued. What you give is just as important as what you get. When two parties have that mindset, there is no limit to how successful the partnership will become!

All that said, it is easy to decide you no longer want to help others because you stand the risk of living your own Golden Goose parable. You should definitely exercise caution. Still, you cannot let the bad behavior of a few bad apples sour your objective to be a leader, trailblazer, philanthropist, mentor and benefactor, or deter you from investing in the well- being of others. And never harbor ill feelings.

That is a toxic state of mind. Don't think too much about the possibility that people who hurt you will somehow "get it back" one day. Not because you are so forgiving, or kind-hearted, but because it is more fulfilling to be thankful for the experiences and people that challenged you. Those trials likely taught you so much about yourself, your potential, and your spirituality. They helped you appreciate the good things a lot more and strengthened you in ways you never imagined. Why would you ever hope that people who helped enlighten you suffer? Besides, we should be so preoccupied with living a better, more promising life that contemplating the fate of those who caused us pain is not even an option. In the words of Napoleon Hill: "The man who does more than he is paid for will soon be paid for more than he does."

6

MICHELLE OBAMA

FINDING YOUR SOUL mate is a goal many people aspire to. They want to connect with a person with whom they will share the rest of their life. And if you are determined to be with someone you are madly in love with then you probably have an image in your mind of *who* that perfect man or woman will resemble. First off, they will get you. Everything about you. They will also be a cheer-leader, advisor, confidant and a partner in innocent mischief. They will be the one who accepts you and all of your shortcomings; who loves you in good times and bad. And above all he or she will remain patient, loyal and strong even as you struggle every day to reach your goals. Ah yes, that one! I can almost see readers' nods of approval as I paint this ideal picture! After all, who would not want this kind of relationship? I will wager, if I were to survey 100 people, more than half (and I'm being conservative) would seize an opportunity to close the deal on a sublime union like the one I just described.

Although the picture I've just painted is not everyone's cup of tea I do believe that most folks are sipping from the same kettle; waiting for the day they get a taste of how pleasurable life will be when they finally meet the "the one."

But before we get lost in this romantic daydream let's take a step back. While everything I've just described sounds extraordinary, in most cases the scenario will only exist in theory. Reality has a way of shining a glaring light on the demanding road that meanders toward this state of bliss. And then, ultimately, the blinding truth is revealed: that life and that person—while it and they may exist—does not come easy. Most of us desire the perfect mate (insomuch as they are perfect to me or you), but we are not willing to do the work it takes to develop a superior relationship once we meet them. Therefore, the fairytale ending hangs in the balance.

A fulfilling life looks spectacular in the present, but if you had a glimpse of the future with all its twists and turns would you still think it is worth having? More often than not we want the dream but we are not willing or prepared to go through the stages necessary to realize it.

Think about it this way: when you settle down to sleep you do not simply lay your head on the pillow and automatically drift off to dreamland. If it were only that easy! There are several phases our brain must go through. When you doze off initially, you sleep very lightly. You then progress deeper and deeper into a dream state. The sleep cycle starts in what's called non–rapid eye movement or NREM stage one. Then you move into a deeper NREM 2 and then to the deepest, NREM 3 (also called slow-wave sleep). Eventually, you experience rapid eye movement (or REM) sleep which is when most of our dreams occur. The whole sequence usually takes somewhere between 90 and 120 minutes. On a typical night you'll cycle through it four or five times, maybe waking up for a second before falling into a state of sleep deep enough to dream. Sometimes, you may even have nightmares. Bottom line, all these functions must occur (ideally uninterrupted) in order to reap the benefits of a good night's sleep. It's an intricate process.

Let me put the scenario of the work it requires to achieve a dream or goal in even more relatable terms. Let's talk about how the life of a person known the world over illustrates how much effort it takes to realize one's dream. Consider the life of Barack Hussein Obama... long before he entered the White House.

Mr. Obama was born to a Caucasian mother from Kansas and a black father from Kenya at a time when interracial relationships were considered taboo. He was raised by his grandfather and his grandmother. Obama's father left the family when Barack was two years old. He died in an automobile accident nineteen years later. Some may have allowed these early challenges to discourage them. Not Mr. Obama. He grew up to become smart and charismatic. The future Commander-in-Chief worked his way through Occidental College in Los Angeles. A degree from Columbia University in New York followed, though neither was an easy endeavor by any means. Remember, he was not a child of privilege. He amassed considerable student loans (although he was fortunate enough to be awarded some scholarships). As he persevered, Obama's focus on political and international affairs remained steady but he often reflected on the isolation he felt. His relationship with his grandfather had always been strained and he did not have his father in his life. Later, he would talk about how the absence of a role model affected him: "I was trying to raise myself to be a black man in America, and beyond the given of my appearance, no one around me seemed to know exactly what that meant." Still, he soldiered on.

In 1985, Barack moved to Chicago where he got his start in community organizing on the city's South Side. He worked to help re-build communities devastated by the closure of local steel plants. According to his biography, his efforts met with some success, but he concluded that, faced with a complex city bureaucracy, "I just can't get things done here without a law degree." In 1988, Obama enrolled at Harvard Law School. He excelled as a student, graduated magna cum laude and was elected president of the prestigious Harvard Law Review for the academic year 1990-1991.

Barack Obama was later elected to the Illinois State Senate in 1996. He called that time in his life "the best education I ever had, better than anything I got at Harvard Law School." He has credited that experience as crucial to finding his identity. It also inspired a dream that would someday lead to the White House. However, that *someday*, would not come easy. He fought hard to make these transitions in his young adult life, often meeting with heavy resistance from colleagues and political foes. While he navigated a road fraught with uncertainty and which would prove mentally draining at times, there was a stable, solid, protective port in the storm: Michelle Robinson, whom he married in 1992.

Today, we know Michelle LeVaughn Robinson Obama as one of the most accomplished women of our time. In addition to being the First Lady of the United States of America, she is a Harvard Law School graduate, Princeton undergrad, a writer and an advocate for poverty awareness, higher education and healthy living. Mrs. Obama has lived in the White House with her husband (the most powerful man in the free world), two beautiful daughters, her Mom and the family's two dogs. She is a world traveler who dines with celebrities and dignitaries and rubs elbows with royalty and world leaders. Mrs. Obama is also friends with celebrities. Safe to say, many women would love to be Michelle Obama. However (and here's the gut check), the Michelle Obama they want to emulate is the woman they see *today*: the elegant, successful, intelligent lady I just described. What most women do not consider is that life for Michelle was not always this way. She did not just happen upon this role people look upon with awe and longing. She earned it. Let's rewind.

Before the inaugurations, state dinners, White House galas and TV interviews, Mrs. Obama was Ms. Michelle Robinson, a young woman born and raised on the South Side of Chicago—the product of hardworking, middle class parents. Thanks to an upbringing accented by love and important life lessons, she too went on to earn a law degree from Harvard University, one the most prestigious institutions in the world. Michelle began working at a Chicago law firm where she would meet and marry a man who dreamt of being the President of the United States. However (as I recounted at length in this chapter), the road to the 1600 Pennsylvania Avenue was not easy.

You must stop and think: before they were married, and shortly thereafter, Michelle had established herself as a powerhouse in her own right, rising through the ranks of corporate America to become the founding director of a federally supported organization, an official in Chicago's City Hall and a respected civil servant. She managed all of this with grace, sophistication and a sense of humor. As Mr. Obama forged a path toward the foreground of American history, Michelle Robinson Obama became the paradigm of a great support system: the woman who willingly sacrificed much of her own life to care for her family while her husband worked countless hours and traveled extensively. Barack, an Illinois State Senator (and eventually a U.S Senator), spent weeks in Washington D.C. working with lawmakers to enact major reforms in healthcare, federal spending oversight and tax legislation. During these days, hours, months and years, Mrs. Obama (in addition to being a practicing attorney and corporate executive) was a full-time doting Mom, a Senator's wife and eventually the President's wife. It's exhausting just thinking about it.

Now, before anyone takes offense to the scenario I have presented make no mistake: I admire Michelle Obama. For several reasons. But no reason stands out more to me than the confidence she exudes. Can you fully comprehend the loyalty, humility, patience and understanding it must have taken to essentially say to the man she loves (at least by her actions): "This is your time and I will do whatever it takes to help you achieve your dreams. Because your dream is *ours*." I can only speculate, but my belief is that she assured Mr. Obama that she had his back no matter what. This woman with a law degree and a mind as sharp and an ambition as intense as her husband's decided that this was the best way to help make a journey that would eventually lead to the White House less arduous. There is nothing like a partner who will sacrifice everything in order to help you achieve something. That can make all the difference in a relationship. It's a blessing. And make no mistake about it, *it is a sacrifice;* one not many people are willing to make.

Michelle was right there with Barack…the entire way. Was it difficult? Of course. Did it put a strain on their marriage? I can't say for sure, however, I don't doubt that kind of pressure wouldn't! For the record, I will bet any amount of money that being the First Lady of the United States is no easy feat. But here's the key: Michelle Obama has the poise to execute her critical role in President Obama's life flawlessly. It is this kind of fierce commitment that sets Mrs. Obama apart.

There is nothing easy about the "fight." The fight to succeed, the fight to keep your family together, the fight to keep your relationship strong no matter the odds. It may sound like some fairytale type of existence where everyone lives happily ever after and oh, by the way, Jay Z and Beyonce are now your best friends. But rest assured, the outcome is hard won. The results are preceded by hardships. The reward is earned, not handed over gratuitously. And through it all, if you do not know who you are—if you are not able to deal with naysayers, saboteurs, critics or just the typical tensions that come with marriage—then quite honestly you are not prepared to be a Mrs. Michelle Obama. You must be self-possessed and selfless. Bold and humble. Extraordinary and laid back. It takes a special kind of person to balance these characteristics.

Mrs. Obama once told a panel hosted by Glamour magazine: "Let's just be clear, you don't want to be with a boy who's too stupid to appreciate a smart young lady. I want to encourage all of us as young women, as older women, we have to raise our own bars." She added: "If I had worried about who liked me and who thought I was cute when I was your age I wouldn't be married to the President of the United States today." That statement is a great example of the premise behind **"The Other 99 T.Y.M.E.S"** If Michelle Obama had submitted to the opinions of all those who tried to break her spirit she would have missed all the good signs that led to her meeting and marrying the person who changed her life forever.

And what does she think about her role as First Lady of the United States? When Barbara Walters asked her that question in an interview just shy of their 20th wedding anniversary, Mrs. Obama replied: "Someone said that there's a perception out there that I feel confined or trapped in some way. To the extent that people have that perception, that couldn't be further from the truth. I feel very blessed in this role."

President Obama never misses an opportunity to praise the woman at his side. In an interview with CNN's Suzanne Malveaux in 2009, Mr. Obama explains why Michelle is his ideal partner. He talks about Michelle's model upbringing (likening it to Ozzie and Harriet). He stresses how important it is knowing she had a stable childhood. A sense of place that was complimentary to his traveling everywhere. He adds that being part of Michelle's family, especially while living in the South Side of Chicago, reassured him that their children would be able to grow up in an embracing family. Mr. Obama once told ABC's Robin Roberts in a Good Morning America exclusive interview, "She puts up with me much more than I expected."

While it takes a great deal to navigate the journey to being Michelle Obama, it takes considerable respect, appreciation and love from her husband, the President, to recognize that she is one of a kind. That she is the exception. Both have been able to see beyond the challenges to recognize all that is good about the other person—everything that brings balance when they are thrown off course. They discovered how each is able to uplift the other when the world tries to tear them down. If either focused on the negativity that they are bombarded with each and every day, instead of the positives that empower their family, there may never have been a Michelle Obama... FLOTUS; one of the greatest role models of our generation.

Ultimately, relationships like the Obamas (and like my parents and grandparents), or perhaps like your own parents or personal unions, are never about what the other person can do for you, but what we can achieve together. When you are in a relationship with the right man/woman, it is not about you. It is about the other person. But here is the catch: that goes both ways. And that is called living THE DREAM! Ask yourself, what do you contribute? What do you bring to the table? What do you do solely for the benefit of the other person? Not because you are going to get something out of it but because you care as much about their needs, dreams and well-being as they do yours.

A deep, meaningful partnership can weather life's greatest storms, bumpiest roads and hardest falls. The best love gets stronger with each struggle. You mature with that kind of love; you learn how to accept, endure, compromise and maintain. You realize it is not all about you. You understand that sometimes you need to bend in order to curve to love. The irony is, if you can be selfless with the right person, you are still rewarded! If you build them up they become stronger. Support them and they can walk more steadily. Appreciate them and who they are apart from you and they know they are respected. Uplift, encourage and honor them, and they will know they are loved. All this will help make them a better person and in turn they are more capable of being the kind of person you want in your corner! What you give is just as important as what you get.

7

PERFECT IMPERFECTIONS

WHEN I FINALLY completed my first book, *"Life Is Not Complicated, You Are"*, the ink on the pages was barely dry before I was flooded with questions from readers, friends and family members inquiring about the topic for the *next* book. Keep in mind; I was still basking in the excitement generated by **"Life Is Not Complicated, You Are"** It was literally a whirlwind. My publicist at Million$Pen, Ink., the company that is also the creative consultant on all my books, was booking interviews, college appearances and book signings. She was organizing a multi-tiered promotional campaign and scheduling speaking engagements faster than we could update the calendar. I was also coming to terms with (and embracing) the peace of mind stemming from the realization that I accomplished what I set out to do, which was to write a book that helped people overcome their challenges. It also enabled me to exorcise my personal demons and come to terms with issues that had weighed me down for years. While I had no clue what the next book would be about, I did know what I did not want the next project to cover: relationships. This was despite the fact that I was bombarded with requests to tackle the topic. A friend of over 20 years even suggested (quite adamantly I might add) a title: "Relationships Are Not Complicated, You Are." I vehemently resisted. I simply did not want to address the topic because relationships are so subjective. Let's face it, what works for one couple does not necessarily suit another. Behaviors that one man or woman might tolerate; others would consider deal breakers. The topic was, to use one of my terms, *complicated*. Even experts agreed. Couples therapist Ellyn Bader wrote: "People have to come to terms with the reality that we really are different people. You are different from who I thought you were or wanted you to be. We have different ideas, different feelings and different interests. It's a stressful—and necessary— evolution. Very complicated,"

After considerable contemplation, I realized it would be impossible to write about *"The Other 99 T.Y.M.E.S"* without addressing the complexities of relationships. Especially since that dynamic is sustained and enriched by the capacity (and willingness) of men and women to appreciate the *"better"* when confronted with the *"worse."* Yes, for better or for worse. This is not just some pithy one-liner that a bride and groom recite during their wedding ceremony. I believe that if couples actually heard and applied the vows in their daily lives instead of just parroting them on the pastor's cue, unions would have more meaning (and longevity). Truth be told, many couples spend more time planning the wedding and the honeymoon than they do preparing for the marriage.

When a couple announces they are getting married, far too often the first response is "let me see the ring." Really? Your first concern after two people have decided to spend the rest of their lives together as husband and wife is how fancy the ring is?

Society as a whole has made the ring the main focus. Celebrities are all over the media highlighting the bling, not the beloved; the carat, not the caring; the sparkle, not the sincerity. Think about it. This suggests love, commitment and passion are measured by the size of a piece of jewelry. If you are building everything you consider meaningful on labels, luxury and lavish lifestyles then you are building your 99 on shaky ground.

Suffice it to say, having considered all of the above, a chapter on relationships became necessary. I wanted to make clear that accepting your partner's imperfections is part of what makes him/her perfect for you; the embodiment of the **Other 99 T.Y.M.E.S**.

To further clarify: when I make reference to relationships, I mean the union between a man and a woman who have chosen a committed bond and respect the obligations this responsibility entails (love, trust, honesty, fidelity and sometimes great personal sacrifice). However, the examples I will expound on can certainly be applied to other relationships including (and not limited to) parent-child, friendships and even employer-employee.

While no one should keep a running tally of "good couple behavior," it is important to recognize when our significant other is doing his or her best. Acknowledge it, appreciate it, file it away in the recesses of your mind where the "why I love him or her chronicles" are stored. When the boundaries of a good relationship are breached and when you become angry, frustrated and disappointed, you can access the experiences and apply the concept of *"The Other 99 T.Y.M.E.S"* Think of the principle as that precise moment you recall everything that makes you love that person: the number of times your partner makes you smile, comforts and supports you. During those times dig deep and shift your focus from whatever bad is happening today, *at this minute,* and appreciate every other day, hour and second that person spends being "the one."

Turbulence during a relationship does not mean its core, foundation and essence changes. Couples will run into obstacles. The challenge may knock the wind out of them, but it does not have to cripple their resolve. Both people must trust that on the other side of crisis still exist the qualities you appreciate. Depending on how long you have been together and how much you value your relationship, the good experiences will likely outnumber the bad. If you are unable

Carlos Wallace and Liz Faublas

to identify enough *T.Y.M.E.S* chances are the problem may lie with you. This is in no way a judgment. It is simply an indication that some introspection may be necessary. As poet Khalid the Future said, "It's not the enemy, it's the inner me." You may discover that ultimately, you are not angry at who your partner is, you are angry at yourself because you expect them to be what *you* want them to be. Trying to change someone to suit your desires is a setup for disappointment. However, this is not necessarily a deal breaker. Dr. Martin Luther King, Jr. said, "We must accept finite disappointment, but never lose infinite hope."

I subscribe to what has been referred to as the "80/20 Rule." Pursuant to this theory, a man or woman in a relationship is getting at least 80 percent of his or her expectations (needs) satisfied. Let's be realistic, that is a considerable majority! Considering the fact that no one is perfect, if you are getting 80 percent of your needs addressed you are well ahead of the game! However, in some situations for whatever reason, some people are still unfulfilled. There is a burning desire to pursue that other twenty percent. That *ratio* is filtered through perception; our minds often see the twenty percent in what appears to be a more attractive package. Perhaps the twenty percent offers a more exciting life dressed up like arm candy you can flaunt at events. Perhaps it lavishes you with extravagant gifts. This sounds perfect but it is still only twenty-percent. That meager quotient does not begin to measure up to what constitutes a whole, fulfilling relationship. Sure, the individual may be more fun and more enticing but that paltry twenty percent he or she brings to the table will never become an adequate investment in your future. These twenty-percenters are not the "responsible, full-day's work with overtime, toil through vacation and sick-days" kind of partners. They are only good for a proverbial 10 p.m. to 2 a.m. "turn up," not a 24-hour guarantee. Pursuing that person therefore is futile and lacks substance. If and when you are faced with the dilemma of choosing one or the other, you must ask yourself where your loyalty (and the best interest of your future) lies.

Is it with the person sharing your bed or with the "gal pal" or "boy toy" you have lunch with for a couple of hours just to vent because they listen to your complaints but have no deeply vested interest in the solution (or you). Consider your answer wisely. Remember, your 80 percent should be your **Other 99 T.Y.M.E.S.**

Relationship expert and professional matchmaker Robin Beltran says one of the biggest issues she's encountered with her clients are unrealistic expectations of relationships, marriage, dating and themselves. Men and women set standards that are unrealistic and border on fantasy. They want perfection when they themselves need "work." And then, when they are paired with someone, they cannot understand why it "just is not right." Over and over again. Robin adds most people have lost sight of the principles and values it takes to sustain a relationship. Most importantly, that it takes work. And it is not always easy, and sometimes you will not like each other. But during those times, you don't jump ship, you weather the storm. If you are not willing to endure difficult times with a person, maybe you are just not ready to be in a relationship.

I remember the days you could share anything with your partner: the embarrassing, the happy, and the sad. I think back to those times and say to myself, there was so much transparency between my grandparents. What they had was so rare, and sincerely special. For sixty-seven years, nothing transpired in their household that husband *and* wife were not privy to. I reflected on this dynamic at length in ***"Life Is Not Complicated, You Are"*** I often wonder what happened to that. Good question, right? Here is an even better question: why not ponder *that* query instead of throwing your hands up and saying "I will just go somewhere else" whenever something goes wrong? Why not explore how the "in it no matter what" aspect of your relationship fizzled out? And once you've asked yourself why, discover a reason (or reasons), and resolve to mend it! Don't make excuses. You must not allow hurt, resentment or misunderstanding to fester even if it means you have to find professional assistance to help with those issues. A relationship is so much easier when you make a conscious decision to accept that *you only have each other.*

That said, problems with your mate should only be discussed within the confines of your union. The opinions of other (non-professionals) are hardly ever objective. Keep in mind, not everything is for everybody. Friends and family should not be privy to the intimate details of your life together, good or bad. Sharing pillow talk with the wrong people can make a hard bed to lie on, and will surely lead to nightmares in your relationship. Part of your **Other 99 T.Y.M.E.S.** should involve taking a step back and noting the respect you have for each other in every circumstance. This respect should be most apparent in the public eye. Say to yourself, "I know I am mad but the world does not have to know." Simply try your best to seek solace in each other.

Ironically (and stay with me here) part of the reason ties are so readily unbound in my opinion is because of misconceptions about the women's equality movement. I am not saying the premise is wrong or ill-conceived. I am a staunch proponent of women's equality; however, when we stop discussing a relationship based on a biblical definition, the premise becomes obscured. These days, the concept has come to mean we do not have to be equally yoked. Instead, it becomes about two independent people who are comfortable enough to say "I don't need to fight. I have enough money to do this on my own! I can take care of myself!" Some women take the whole girl power, Beyonce "to the left" theme to an entirely disturbing level. Independence does not mean defiance, especially when you are sharing your life with someone.

Generations ago, couples had to stay together. The man was the primary provider. He brought home the income and Mother ran the house. In some cases, Dad had no idea where the pots and pans were kept, much less how to prepare an entire meal. Just the thought of the struggle that awaited you if you didn't have your partner was incentive enough to work out your differences. Adversity and challenges made relationships stronger; they brought out the true depth of love. Time was taken to consider all that was good and worthwhile before someone bailed out. Today, the options abound: opportunities are more available. Marriage gets put off to a later date. A 2012 study by the Brookings Institute shows that as women have gained more economic control over their lives, they have been offered more choices than they had just a few decades ago. Opportunities in the workplace have allowed women to become more financially independent, making marriage less of an economic necessity. Unfortunately, it seems knowing we have an easy way out weakens our resolve and diminishes the bond.

Issues can only be resolved if each person accepts accountability and embraces their role in the union. There is always enough blame to go around. Find traits in yourself you can repair to make the situation better. This will have a profound, positive impact on the 80 percent! If you cannot identify your own faults, you will definitely struggle to repair the relationship. Honestly, we are all judgmental. We may not want to admit we are because we are so self-righteous. You need only read the first book of the New Testament to understand we are born into that kind of sin. For most people shaking the habit is difficult.

Unfortunately, no matter how hard a couple works at focusing on *"The Other 99 T.Y.M.E.S"*, it may not always work out. As a divorced man, I can say from experience that there may come a time when a couple decides it is best to live separate lives: where you have different dreams and are no longer willing to make sacrifices to achieve the other's goal. If a person begins to chip away at who you are, you need to extricate yourself from that toxic environment. The choice for me was simple. I am not built to be sub-par. I give 100% to every aspect of my life. I could no longer do that in my marriage. I preferred to be a divorced man than a bad husband.

Relationships should never be completely about what the other person can do for you. Ask yourself, what do you contribute? What do you bring to the table? What do you do solely for the benefit of the other person? Not because you are going to get something out of it, but because you care as much about their needs, dreams, and well-being as they do yours. The irony is, if you can be selfless with the right person, you are still rewarded! If you build them up, they become stronger. Support them and they can walk more steadily. Appreciate them and who they are apart from you, and they will know they are respected. Uplift, encourage and honor them and they will know they are loved. All this will help make them a better person and in turn they will be more capable of being the kind of person you want in your corner! What you give is just as important as what you get. When both people have that mindset, there is no limit to how successful your union will become! This is when you will see your 80 percent move closer to the 100 percent mark…simply becoming perfect imperfections!

O'Neal & Elnora Hunt
(Early Years)

8

BITTERSWEET

THE TITLE OF this chapter is very meaningful to me. I will go so far as to say these pages may represent the heart and soul of the entire book— the driving force behind its concept.

Let me begin by stating I will never write a book that requires more of the reader than he or she is willing (or has time) to give. I've learned throughout my life that the more we complicate things the less people are inclined to participate. I don't judge anyone for adopting that mindset. If you read my last book, *"Life Is Not Complicated, You Are"*, you know I am a staunch advocate for keeping our thoughts, actions and interactions as simple as possible, without compromising meaning and substance. Simplicity should never translate to mundane.

That said, I compel everyone reading this book to ask themselves simple yet meaningful questions. I encourage you to look deep into your heart and explore the recesses of your mind to understand the *why*. Look beyond the "what," the "who" or the "how." These are surface questions that usually require one or two word responses and little reflection. Instead, consider: *Why* do you feel the way you do? *Why* do you choose to focus on the negative rather than see the bright side? *Why* are you compelled to nurse your pain rather than nurture your joy? When faced with the choice (and it is **always** a choice) of being angry, disappointed or sad about our lot in life versus being encouraged, thankful and content why do so many of us choose the former? We are all capable of regulating how we think and feel. It just boils down to owning that power. Confidently. Even defiantly in some cases. Decide to train your mind to see the good in all things, no matter how bad they appear on the surface. Amanda Chen, Managing Editor of Healthy Living, provided one of the most accurate list of habits attributable to people who never worry. The ones that stand out most with me:

- They focus on the present
- They are more willing to take chances
- They have a sense of perspective
- They get to the root of the worry
- They have confidence they can handle whatever comes at them
- They have the ability to see positive outcomes in seemingly bleak situations
- They know how to perceive their negative emotions

These habits are actionable. They are controllable. There is nothing more empowering than sizing up a situation and deciding, in no uncertain terms, that you are stronger than your challenges. Mind over matter is not a myth. It is a reality that everyone has at their disposal.

Chen writes that while everyone worries from time to time, it *is* possible to worry so much that it starts to have a noticeable impact on your daily life. Getting a grasp on the strategies she listed will help break the cycle of negativity and non-progressive thinking.

One of the greatest men I have ever known (and may ever know) in my life is my father, Aaron Lee Wallace, Jr. Many friends and acquaintances were surprised to learn that he was actually my stepfather. That is because to me, this was always a distinction without a difference. Aaron Wallace loved me as his son, and I loved him as my father, and that is all that mattered. We were not limited by formal labels. Our connection to one another transcended accepted familial classifications. What we lacked in DNA we more than made up for in love, respect and the understanding that as I long as I live I am a Wallace—Carlos Wallace, son of Aaron and Alice. That's who I am, period. Still, people ask, "What about your biological father? Don't you ever wonder where he is or what kind of life you would have had if you were in touch?" The short answer is no, I don't at all. Ever. There was never a need to ponder it. There was *never a need* to look for, talk about, resent or have any feeling whatsoever about my biological father because the man who raised us provided me with everything I could ever need. I believed wholeheartedly that if I wasted a moment thinking about the man my mother was with before Aaron Lee then I had lost sight of my **Other 99 T.Y.M.E.S**. If I did that, then I would be questioning a definite for a maybe; I would be pondering a possible outcome when I had an actual reality. Why would I complicate a life that, for all intents and purposes, was ideal? I practiced what I preached and asked myself a tough question: why should I go looking for an absentee father, when I had a father who was present, dedicated and caring? I chose to "uncomplicate" things!

We pursue senseless outcomes sometimes. Even when we know what is right and reasonable. For instance, I did not obsess about getting to know my biological father because my rationale was this: if you matter to someone, you will know it. Spending hours, days and weeks of your valuable time wondering if someone is thinking about you, cares about you and wants you in his or her life should be a reasonable indication that he or she probably does not. In the meantime, you are ignoring the people who do not hesitate to show their love. It is important, however, to remember that some people are oblivious and have no clue they are not sending the right messages. If you want them bad enough, speak up. Maybe they just need a wake-up call. Still, (I can't stress this enough) if they are thinking about you, they should let you know. If they care about you, you will feel it. If they want you in their life (and you want them in yours), they will open the door with open arms and welcome you. Your value in another person's life is not negotiable. It is not up for discussion. Set the standard and stick to it. Above all, make sure you acknowledge the people who willingly invest their time in your well-being.

One of the most glaring examples of this principle is the relationship between my mother and father. A more unlikely pair never exist-ed! Yet the story of their courtship and 67 years of marriage will serve as the benchmark for what it means to sacrifice for another person—to appreciate the wealth of goodness a person can bring to one's life in spite of the many challenges that life brings.

My mother was diagnosed with childhood diabetes at age nine. Doctors said her chances of living to adulthood were slim and even that prognosis was optimistic. What's more, she was warned that should she survive, she could forget about having children. The risks to an already fragile body would be too great. Yet, in spite of all these warnings, the prospect of a future with a sickly wife, a future filled with medical bills and doctor's visits, the possibility their marriage would be short-lived, my father took Alice Novel Hunt as his wife, for better or worse, in sickness and in health. And he meant every

(l) Step Wallace (age 3), (tl) Carlos Wallace (age 6), (bl) Aurelia Wallace (age 1), © Alice Wallace, ® Aaron Lee Wallace, Jr.

single word. You see, it was more important to my father to be with a woman who brought him more joy than sadness. He would rather revel in years of bliss than regret buckling to fears about a few days of discomfort. I must add that my mother was quite stubborn. She went on to carry four pregnancies to full-term. Alice Wallace saw all her children become adults. She took four chances that brought her the greatest joy of her life, rather than make one decision (to avoid having children) that she would have regretted forever.

Our lives are filled with countless examples that emphasize the concept of this chapter. My personal life is full of them. However, this book is about engaging the reader. Making sure he or she finds answers by assessing the world around them and by surveying their own lives. Let's examine a story outside the Wallace household.

Alonzo Spellman was arguably one of the most controversial football players of his generation. During his nine-year NFL career, he played for the Chicago Bears, Dallas Cowboys and Detroit Lions. He was a man with phenomenal potential but marginal ambition: an athlete whose talent (and fate) for years remained suspended between the two realities. He was known for his massive size, brute force and propensity to roll over opponents like a freight train—a hulking mass of physical power that made him a force to be reckoned with on the football field. The trouble was, he was not able to control this aggressive, barbaric behavior off the gridiron. He was given to random, extreme acts of violence and vicious verbal attacks. He was also prone to suicidal thoughts. It soon became apparent there was something terribly wrong with this young man. The diagnosis was disturbing yet came as a surprise to no one: Spellman suffered from bipolar disorder, a mood disorder characterized by mood swings from mania (exaggerated feeling of well-being, stimulation, and grandiosity in which a person can lose touch with reality) to depression (overwhelming feelings of sadness, anxiety, and low self-worth, which can include suicidal thoughts and suicide attempts). Doctors were able to treat his illness with medication, but that salve came at a price. Medication soothed the savage beast and at the same time tamed the raging player. Various reports suggested Spellman battled a dilemma more troublesome than his illness. Should he continue taking drugs to manage his aggression? Or forego treatment to play with the intensity that made him a notable sports figure? None of this even mentions the difficulty he must have had contending with the stigma attached to mental illness. In speaking about Chicago Bears wide receiver Brandon Marshall who was diagnosed with borderline personality disorder, ESPN.com sports writer, Marin Cogan, explains, "In the NFL, where admitting even physical damage to the brain was long thought to be a shameful sign of weakness, to have someone of Marshall's status be forthcoming about an invisible, non-trauma-induced brain issue is borderline miraculous. There could be perhaps no more difficult, and populist, an institution for the mental health community to take on."

While Marshall has been able to manage his condition and enjoy a successful pro-football career while being a spokesperson for BPD, for Spellman, confronting the demons head-on proved too overwhelming. For a brief period in 2006 he accepted that he needed to take his daily medication in order to calm the urge toward erratic and dangerous behavior. He was able to control the disease enough that after a five-year absence, he played football again. It did not take long for redemption to turn (once again) into darkness. By choosing not to medicate (and it was a choice), Spellman decided to live with the rage under the delusion he was ok. He expected the NFL to accept him as he was instead of undergoing treatment that would alter his personality and perhaps the league's perception of his ability as an athlete. In Spellman's case, he could not find a balance; he could not find an acceptable method of appreciating the positive effects consistent treatment would bring about. He settled into the chaos of a world darkened by mental illness. As with other examples of *"The Other 99 T.Y.M.E.S"*, this shows our choices have consequences. Sometimes, those consequences are not favorable.

Some of my dearest friends are comics, poets, writers, and corporate professionals. A few have shared that they have been diagnosed with depression. When I ask why they don't take medication for the disease, one close friend confided, "It would dim my light. I would be walking in a fog. It would numb my senses and curb my creativity. All I have is my art and my talent. It's the one thing I am sure of. My ability to write and perform is my solace even in my darkest moments. True insanity, to me, would mean I'd no longer be able to escape into my passion. If I lose that, I might as well be dead." She suffers. It hurts to see her struggle. But she's made her choice. She'd rather be tortured for 99 days and enjoy the gifts she's been blessed with than drift through a life of mind-numbing stability. Bittersweet.

I am often told (typically by people who have trouble embracing an optimistic attitude), that my approach to life is "easier said than done." I don't think people who choose to think positively or who maintain an optimistic attitude about life have all the answers. Honestly, I don't even think life was meant to be "figured out." It's in a constant state of flux. My faith tells me that you are given this gift from the Creator. You have the free will to do with it as you like. You can allow life to "just happen" around you; you can chose to allow it to exist without any order. However, bear in mind that uncertainty typically leads to discontent.

Alternatively, you can experience life as a journey of discovery. You can participate, explore, probe and inquire. You can ask yourself questions: Why am I sad? Why am I happy? Why am I stalled? Why is it important that I make a difference? Why do I need to improve my life? Why do I need to progress? Why am I hurting? Why did I turn to that individual? Why am I not moving on to my next phase of learning? Why am I on this leg of my journey at this time? It is about asking the right questions. Enlightenment flows like water: it assumes the shape of the moment, your thoughts, and the soul. When you are adrift on life's choppy waters, just follow the rolling waves of your questions until you settle into a reservoir of peace and acceptance. Then, drop anchor.

Life will always have some bitter aspects to it, but it's the sweetness of it all that allows us to see beyond the surface!

9

GAME DAY

WHEN YOU GROW up in Texas, the love of football is almost second nature. There are a few exceptions to that generally accepted principle, however, you will be hard-pressed to find many Texans who do not have at least a general interest in the game. Admittedly, as a child I *preferred* basketball. That was because my mother had effectively mastered the sport and instilled her deep love of the game in me. You might recall, I was born moments after my mother had played one of the greatest basketball games of her entire collegiate career. It stands to reason that as far as I am concerned, from that moment on (and as soon as I could handle the rock), it seemed as if I was destined to dribble a basketball. I admire the sport as one of finesse, endurance and critical thinking: mind and body must be in tune.

As I've gotten older—and since my mother's death—I still appreciate a game of basketball, but I've turned much of my attention to football. My love for and understanding of the game gets keener with each season. As with most interests in my life, I study the sport. I know its history. I understand the mechanics and the nuances. Basically, I've learned just about every aspect of the sport. So much so that I am able to draw upon its makeup and use it as one of my favorite (and most effective) metaphors about life. It's become one of those signature analogies that I share with friends and family that leaves them wondering: how does this guy come up with this stuff? And in most cases, people agree with the comparisons I expound upon, especially when I am engaged in a conversation about a team or a business.

Simply put, when you stop and think about the game of a football, the goal of every play is to score. Each team's objective is to outperform, outwit and out play the opponent—and of course to win the game no matter what. It's about strategy and execution. Another important component is the occasional (unplanned) audible. For example, the offense is facing a third and short and the quarterback identifies that the play called will not outmatch the defensive strategy he is facing, so the quarterback calls an audible. Ultimately, all's fair (and quite possible) in the heat of the game. No matter the call, there will never be a play designed to fail. If there is ever a question or hint of doubt, the play is deliberated upon and relayed to the men on the field very decisively, often times by the offensive coordinator who is typically located way up in a skybox overlooking the field. And what a view that is! He can see things those at eye-level do not have the advantage of seeing. Stop and think about the pressure he is under; the intense mind game he is processing from his vantage point of the gridiron. This man is literally engaged in a cerebral chess match. His opponent? The defensive coordinator on the opposite team—an adversary that has challenged him to summon up his best plays and his most precise strategy. The defensive coordinator is a rival that is expecting him to read his mind. And he, this offensive coordinator on whose decisions the entire game hangs, must do all he can to ensure he calls the play that will counter what he believes his opponent is prepared to defend. After seconds of precision planning, he sends the highly anticipated signal to the sideline and that play, that critical interpretation of his strategy, is communicated to the quarterback, who, in the huddle, will call the intended play. He's got a set time to assure that each of the ten players understand the role each must assume in the designated play. All things equal and executed without error, each lineman will make the correct block, the receivers will run the proper

Carlos Wallace (age 15)

route, and/or the running back will take the handoff and hit the gap just right. If everything goes as planned, the desired outcome will be reached: touchdown. Here is where the analogy begins to unfold.

The player that scores the touchdown becomes a hero—the focus of every single person watching that game for about seven to 10 seconds. He takes a moment to savor a play successfully carried out, but only for a moment. Because when he completes his ritualistic touchdown dance and reality overrides the roar of the crowd, he remembers (or at least he should) that it's back to the sidelines he goes. The game continues. The team must kickoff and prepare to play defense. And even when the clock ticks down to the final seconds and the game ends, the cycle I just described continues throughout the season. The team must win enough games to reach the Super Bowl. And once *that* game is over, it's time to start all over again and prepare for next year.

The most important message I want the reader to derive from this play-by-play is, it's not about who won the game or how. While all these games unfold and teams bask in the glow of victories (which hopefully exceed losses), team members must not lose sight of one very key aspect of the entire process: none of this would be possible were it not for the calculated, unified, orchestrated efforts of an entire team. And not just a team, but an entire organization. I mean, everyone from the secretaries that answer the phones in the corporate office, to the trainers that tape up weakened ankles, to the physician that rushes to the field when a player is down, to the wives and family members who support the players throughout the season during every game win or lose. The concerted effort of the entire organization made that epic success on the field possible. Moreover, everyone has to be secure enough in his or her role in the organization to understand that, regardless of how big or small your assigned tasks, the mission could not have been completed without everyone's contribution. HRbible.com explains that teamwork in any organization is important and essential for it to succeed. For an organization to achieve its goals, it needs to run like a well-oiled machine composed of different parts working together. Teamwork becomes the oil that makes everything keep running smoothly in any organization or company.

Additionally, one must take each game as it comes. There will be bad seasons. Do not let that take away from the extraordinary ones. You must not let losses convince you that the career you've worked so hard to build (which has had its share of wins) is now over. You must not rest on the laurels of a banner season or winning game. Nor must you be derailed by a losing one.

I apply the football analogy to every aspect of my life where I am part of a team or a group of individuals that have come together for a common goal: the success of the whole. It's a discipline I practice in my own company, Sol-Caritas. I may be the CEO, but I understand that every vice president, every artist and every production assistant, every freelancer and ticket buyer contributes to growth of the organization. When one member is weak or not wholly committed to the betterment of the team, it sends a ripple effect that resonates throughout the enterprise. Author and businessman John C. Maxwell said, "Teamwork is always at the heart of great achievement. The question isn't whether teams add value. The question is whether we will acknowledge that fact and work to become better team players." All this also requires consistency. You can't be engaged and excited one day because everything is going gangbusters and then fall back a week, a month or a year later because your interest is no longer piqued. At that point you must ask what happened to the passion that drove your desire and work ethic. What happened to the times when you were grateful for the job and the opportunity? When did passion and gratitude turn into the moaning and complaining about going to work or having to put in "extra time" on a project leaving you unable to hang out with friends and family? In the end, what makes individuals lose complete sight of the **Other 99 T.Y.M.E.S** when the task at hand meant the world to them? I'll tell you: complacency, lack of gratitude and focusing on the bad day or the office worker you do not like or the disappointment of missing out on the football game or not being able to attend your child's recital or take a vacation. I am not suggesting any of those things are not important to an individual. I am simply calling attention to the fact that at one time, it was more important to feed your family, have access to health insurance and pay your bills than it was to meet up with friends and hang out. At one point you said, "This is a blessing, a priority, and I have to make sacrifices." It's easy to forget this, turn around and say I hate that I have to sacrifice so much for "this job." So the job that saved your life stopped being a blessing? Why?

When I applied for a position in the rail industry the company I submitted my application to explained that they interview and vet 500 people. After a selective screening process potential candidates gather in a large conference room. The company's representative announces, "If we call your name, please proceed to the appointed representative standing by. If we do not, you will be asked to leave at the end of the roll call and will be free to apply once again in six months." Imagine being among hundreds of men and women looking around at each candidate and praying "Please let me be the one to make the cut." Each of them hoping they would be among the chosen few who got to step up to the "appointed representative" that held the key to their future employment. At the end of this nerve-wrecking process, they hired up to ten men and women. Speaking from personal experience, the only thing that mattered at that time was, "If I am among the ten, I will be so grateful." And as I vowed, I did remain grateful for that job until my last day working for the railroad.

Thanks to the guidance and experience of my father A. L. Wallace, Jr. (a.k.a. Bigfoot), a man who dedicated over thirty years to the railroad industry, I am a fifth generation railroader. I also understand (because of my father's direction) that most personal conflicts with a company have nothing to do with its rules and objectives. Those guidelines exist from day one; put into effect the moment the company is established! There are no surprises. They are often modified over time however, the general principles are hard and fast. For instance, in the rail industry working holidays and long hour moving freight are normal occurrences. There are no exceptions. It only becomes an issue when it conflicts with the employee's personal agenda. My question is, when did it become more about your personal needs and less about the expectations of the company that employs you? The organization that hired you instead of 490 others that day…remember that? You prayed and promised to be thankful if you were given the opportunity. At what point did it become justifiable to complain about the job because it keeps you later (in order to meet a deadline) than you typically work? You conveniently overlook the fact that this job also provided the insurance that helped pay for your wife's breast cancer treatment. You lament that you are frustrated because you were not given the day off for your birthday and forget that you were approved for days that exceeded typical, lawfully allotted bereavement leave to allow you extra time to mourn your mother's death. When did the company's primary initiative (conducting business under the appointed guidelines you agreed to comply with) become a hassle? I am not saying your personal life is not important. It is very important. To *you*. As for the company you work for, they set their goals long before you began working there and will keep those objectives long after you leave. That goal is important to *them*. That simply will not change, especially not to accommodate your personal plans. But somehow the **Other 99 T.Y.M.E.S** that company has come through for you mean so little. I can assure you that there is someone without a job who would love to provide for his or her family and take care of their medical needs and who would love to walk in your shoes the **Other 99 T.Y.M.E.S** *as well as* the ONE time beyond that.

Vince Lombardi is one of America's most famous football coaches. He was the assistant coach for the New York Giants from 1954 to 1958 and served as Head Coach for the Green Bay Packers of the National Football League. He led the Packers to five league championships during his nine years as coach, 1959 to 1967. One of my favorite quotes comes courtesy of this great leader and is the perfect summation to the chapter: "People who work together will win, whether it be against complex football defenses or the problems of modern society."

Ultimately, you do not have to be a football fanatic to appreciate that the lessons learned on game day can become a valuable blueprint for life.

10

PAIN MANAGEMENT

DEPRESSION. YES, I said it.

I understand it is a difficult condition to talk about. I acknowledge it is an illness many prefer not to discuss at all. I know many of you may even be tempted to flip the pages and read ahead to the next chapter. Just the very mention of the word dredges up all the stigmas, fears and misunderstanding about depression. Honestly, before I began writing the chapter I thought that maybe I should camouflage the topic with a funny story, dramatization or inspiring quote. Pour a little sugar on a subject that typically leaves a bad taste in one's mouth, in much the same way your mom would disguise that bitter medicine by sweetening it with honey or tucking it away under your favorite food. Dupe you into ingesting it because she knew it was good for you; that you needed it in order to get better. However, I've come to learn from experience that it does not matter *how* a message is delivered; it matters more *that* it is delivered. And sometimes it resonates more deeply without the bells and whistles that may drown out the truth.

As I explained in an earlier chapter and in *"Life Is Not Complicated, You Are"*, one is more capable of bearing the weight of depression when they accept that there is an issue in the first place and are reassured that they are not alone in fighting the battle. Pain Management is intended to show the reader how focusing on the **Other 99 T.Y.M.E.S** can help ease the burden of depression. The next few pages will highlight the lives of people who have discovered ways to cope.

We've talked about the trials and triumphs of NFL player Marshall Brandon. His story epitomizes how someone can find hope; that it is possible to turn on the proverbial light and find a way out of the mind's darkness. In an article published in the Huffington Post, Marshall bravely admits to the way he struggled to control his emotions and manage his life and relationships. He adds that as a longtime athlete in the NFL (which in his words he describes as a "testosterone-driven, tough-it-up, egocentric profession"), there's not a lot of room for, "Hey, guy, so how are you feeling today?"

So what finally convinced him to seek help? Marshall recalls becoming extremely isolated and depressed. He stopped speaking to his wife and family. He turned in on himself. This behavior became the new normal. But it was not a feeling he wanted to bask in. He needed to find out why he felt there was such an oppressive weight on his life: like he was being pulled underwater, gasping for air with no will to fight. Finally, Marshall went to McLean Hospital (near Boston) where he was diagnosed with a mental disorder and received a treatment plan that transformed his life. When asked why it took so long to get help, Marshall recounted a common deterrent: the stigma surrounding mental illness. Once he came to grips with that reality, he was inspired to start a foundation to raise awareness, erase the stigma, and help people get diagnosed and treated for depression.

One of the key elements of Marshall's treatment, which relates directly to the concept of the **Other 99 T.Y.M.E.S**, is the principle of "radical acceptance," which he says taught him to accept the world as it is. He learned that everything bad he'd ever done, everything people had done to him, each time he hurt someone or had been hurt —he needed to let go. He had to treat himself and others with compassion. He also had to stop trying to change the past. This last aspect of his awareness is so profoundly tied to the message I am trying to convey. There is so much "now" to be embraced and appreciated. There is the promise of new opportunities and new days to become a better person (husband, wife, child, athlete or entertainer). There are the **Other 99 T.Y.M.E.S** to be appreciated and enjoyed. But you have to want to break free from the shackles of sadness and discouragement. Marshall Brandon wanted freedom and he did what he needed to do to find it: pain management.

In *Lincoln's Melancholy: How Depression Challenged a President and Fueled His Greatness*, biographer Joshua Wolf Shenk writes, "Humor gave Lincoln protection from his mental storms. It distracted him and gave him relief and pleasure . . . Humor also gave Lincoln a way to connect with people." Shenk goes on to write that the "President's coping strategies ultimately helped him lead the nation through its greatest turmoil." Rather than give in to his illness, he realized his greater purpose. Instead of succumbing to the struggle, President Lincoln focused on his **Other 99 T.Y.M.E.S** and changed the course of this country's history: pain management.

Sigmund Freud is the father of psychoanalysis, a clinical method for treating psychopathology through dialogue between a patient and a psychoanalyst. Ironically, he also suffered from depression. Now, Freud's **Other 99 T.Y.M.E.S** stand in stark contrast to Marshall and Lincoln, but I believe many people will relate to what forced this genius to look past his illness. While many credit Freud's lengthy self-analysis as an effective treatment, it also appears that recognition by the world was a powerful depression antidote. Freud, at an early age, very much wanted fame and acknowledgement. The need to have one's work, life and accomplishments acknowledged is a powerful motivator for some! In this case, it encouraged one of the world's greatest minds to escape from his emotional and mental prison: pain management.

I can go on for pages with similar examples, but you get the point by now. Once you make the decision to re-evaluate, reconsider and re-train the way you think, process experiences and relate to the people around you, the healing can begin.

This in no way is intended to simplify the severity of depression. Sometimes it takes years of treatment to find relief. The common thread among all these survivors is that their depression did not stem from a "bad day." The condition is so much deeper than a fleeting moment of melancholy because you are not able to appreciate the good in your life; therefore, all the times circumstances worked in your favor mean nothing. A few bouts of disappointment effectively removed the bloom from the rose. That is, until the next *favorable* outcome comes along and all is right with the world.

In my close, personal experience with someone who has been diagnosed with clinical depression, I know firsthand that the sadness lingers even when they hit the jackpot, live in a mansion, work at a dream job, have the best-behaved children, or find a loving relationship. There is no distinction between what makes them happy or sad. It's all a blur. When they are able to think clearly, perhaps in their quiet moments, when they can take a long, honest look at their life (past and present) in order to realistically examine relationships with others and with themselves, and begin to admit that on some level they are broken, that is when they take one of the biggest steps toward changing their outlook. Understandably, the term broken is laced with pejorative undertones. Even that stigma, as in the case of Brandon Marshall, is one of the reasons I believe some people do not take that journey to the bottom of their heart or souls;: people have convinced themselves that being "broken" or "damaged" means you are weak or somehow unstable. That is not the case. The strongest among us are those who are able to admit we are human and we hurt. It means you are not hiding from your fears or insecurities. Instead you are confronting them head on and accepting the challenge of curing what ails your heart and soul. With this mindset, you have begun to free yourself from the "monsters" that haunt and limit you. You are looking away from the "abyss" and toward the light. It's a leap of faith. You have to trust God and yourself, and know in your heart and mind that when you take that leap, He will not allow you to fall. According to Nietzsche, *"Whoever fights monsters should see to it that in the process he does not become a monster. And if you gaze long enough into an abyss, the abyss will gaze back into you."*

The point I want to drive home is, no matter how difficult the road to recovery may seem, you can get there if you set your sights on the good in your life, on the people who love you, and on your dreams. You can do this one minute at a time, one hour at a time, and one day at a time. You are not alone. You can do what so many others have. You can survive, with your own powerful form of pain management.

Ultimately, I am not an authority on depression or social sciences, nor do I purport to have all the answers about either. But I do know that people very close to me sometimes live in darkness. Sometimes I feel so helpless because I am not able to help them, but I always remind them they are not alone and that darkness is not permanent. However, they have to want to "turn the light on." They have to want to pick themselves up, and find a reason to live for. They have to seek out the things that matter, and realize that if they disappear, others will hurt: kids, spouses, parents and friends.

One of the greatest, most valuable lessons my mother taught me and that I discuss throughout *"Life Is Not Complicated, You Are"* is simply that I matter. No matter my circumstances, no matter the opinion of others, no matter my struggles, and, quite frankly, no matter how successful I become, nothing should define me more than my own opinion of myself. My mom taught me to know my worth and my value and to realize I deserve happiness, love and understanding. These things mean so much more when it comes from within first. When all is said and done, self-love is one of the most effective forms of pain management.

11

IGNORED INFLUENCE

ON AUGUST 14, 2015, the American biographical dramatic film, *"Straight Outta Compton,"* was released. The movie, directed by F. Gary Gray, chronicles the rise and fall of Compton, California hip hop group N.W.A. ("Niggaz Wit Attitudes"). The biopic, which garnered critical acclaim, grossed over $200 million dollars worldwide and sparked a debate that had people on both sides of the issue opin-ing on the negative and positive effects of hip hop on society. The group's provocative, unapologetic verses challenged authority and gave a powerful, defiant voice to the disenfranchised throughout one of America's most dangerous cities. Their signature track, *"Fuck the Police,"* breathed vindication into the embattled souls of a generation. It became an anthem for the economically paralyzed living in similar low-income, high-crime communities around the country. Whether or not you agreed with the group's incendiary style, one thing most people will agree on: N.W.A had a deep, transformative and lasting effect on hip hop ideology. I believe hip hop's characteristic beliefs as a whole are misunderstood, underappreciated and highly under-estimated. Tupac, Biggie Smalls, Rakim, Pimp C, Nas, Slim Thug, Jay Z, Eminem, Run DMC, Kanye West, Lauryn Hill, MC Lyte—no mat-ter who is deemed a groundbreaking artist—one thing remains in-disputable, hip hop continues to be society's ignored influence. The misconception is that the genre is a breeding ground for negativity;

that it is the birthplace of violence and misogynistic attitudes, and the genesis of every kind of unfavorable stereotype imaginable. When, in fact, if looked at through the lens of neutrality and open-mindedness, the virtues of hip hop far outweigh the negative stigma attached to it.

A lot has changed in the quarter century since the world was first introduced to N.W.A. Hip hop in its purest form has evolved, inspired, educated and created a lucrative independent revenue stream for what was once a poverty-stricken, hopeless class of artists. Let's examine hip hop's **Other 99 T.Y.M.E.S**.

The music (and the entire category) is one of few that unites fans of all colors, races, religions, socio-economic backgrounds, ages and genders. I remember attending the Jay Z and Beyoncé concert in New York. As I surveyed the arena I was blown away by the diversity of the crowd. Lovers of rap music in all forms convened for a singular reason: their appreciation of hip hop. I've sat in the bleachers at college football games and witnessed firsthand men and women, black, white, brown and of varying ages bobbing their heads and mouthing the words to *"Niggas In Paris"* when they broadcast the song inside the arena between plays. Much of this cohesiveness can be attributed to the music's multi-cultural roots. According to a study conducted by the Oxford African American Studies Center, hip hop is part of and speaks to a long line of black American and African traditions. Many observers also make a connection between rap and West African griot tradition, the art of wandering storytellers known for their knowledge of local settings and their superior vocal skills. We must also take into account the influences of R&B, funk, soul, jazz, rock and roll, poets, and what many might consider an unlikely source: the black church. Black preachers and clergy combined testimonials and parables in a way that engaged the audience and brought their sermons to life.

Radio and talk show host, advocate and philanthropist, Tavis Smiley, offered a salient explanation of this theory. "Since hip hop emerged from the South Bronx in the 1970s, it has become an international, multi-billion-dollar phenomenon. It has grown to encompass more than just rap music. Hip hop has created a culture that incorporates ethnicity, art, politics, fashion, technology and urban life." This debunks the widely accepted argument that the genre is inherently divisive. With so many factors converging to create such an intricate, informative and multi-faceted genre, whose history and impact have bridged barriers between artist and society, it is not too complicated an endeavor to understand that its relevance repudiates its notorious reputation.

We listen to rap lyrics, but few study the history. One of the most significant contributions of hip hop? It offers a profound social commentary on the black experience. This is an aspect of the music that is overlooked because most people choose to pay more attention to "the hook" (the catchy repetitive phrase) than the complete body of work. In doing so, the listener misses the message: the essence of the music, the breakdown of the bars. That's tantamount to someone who is able to quote scripture, but has never read the bible. You are only getting snippets of a greater message. You think you understand the origins of the faith when in fact you have barely skimmed its legacy. Therefore, you cannot speak credibly about the religion. As millions use social media as a primary source of information, the risk of falling victim to being misinformed is high. Readers who quickly scan newsfeeds tend to only read (and share information about) a headline: focusing on "the hook." Whether due to complacency or lack of time, few explore the content. This allows bogus media outlets to descend on the unsuspecting (and unprepared) seekers of instant information, creating false stories with dazzling one-liners, secure in the knowledge that there will be little effort to pursue confirmation or research an entire story. Your ability to tell the real story is stymied. Your voice is limited. As evidenced in these examples, this method of consuming information is pointless. Cursory translations of hip hop also will not help anyone fully grasp its meaning. To embrace hip hop and its entire message (listening beyond the hook), means finally having a voice—a complete and empowered voice. The OAASU article I referenced earlier breaks it down even more acutely:

Comedians such as Richard Pryor, Redd Foxx, and Flip Wilson influenced the development of hip hop by using their gifts of oration to bring the style, rhythms, and stories of the streets into their comedic narratives. Like people playing the dozens, these comedians used humor to shock and provoke, at the same time imbuing their narratives with a knowing social commentary that reflected the black experience. As entertainers they told stories that the everyday person could understand but punctuated it with a style that was unique to black America. Early rap musicians used these and other oratorical techniques to impart knowledge and entertain through rhymed verses that form narratives. This interweaving of vocal skills and storytelling traditions affected how rap was produced and what was said in the lyrics, giving rise to a new expressive culture that reflected the social conditions of the day.

This is a form of expression that gives a generation, once ignored and condemned to failure, an outlet to tell their story. If we view hip hop in this manner, it becomes crystal clear what one stands to gain by understanding the genre, and that it outweighs what critics claim is lost by listening to the music.

If you do not believe that hip hop crosses barriers, consider this term: *"Cultural appropriation."* I first came across the term while reading a 2015 Boston Globe article. It's a label that has been attributed to artists like Elvis and Pat Boone who recreated figuratively pale versions of early rock n' roll classics by Little Richard and Fats Domino. The concern centered on not only who makes the music, but who claims its legacy and shapes its future. The term was reincarnated when rapper Macklemore, who is white, and his musical partner, Ryan Lewis, won four Grammys in 2014 (including best rap album, rap song, and rap performance), felt compelled to say that as a white man he knows he must tread respectfully in a genre created by and still dominated by African-Americans.

The business of hip hop is probably the most tangible example of the genre's dramatic maturation. A quick look at a 2015 Forbes article entitled **The Forbes Five: Hip Hop's Wealthiest Artists of 2015** is further illustration of how the culture's most successful artists have advanced the culture beyond the music. After calculating current holdings, past earnings and discussions with various analysts and other industry experts and players, Forbes writer, Zack O'Malley Greenberg, author of **Empire State of Mind: How Jay Z Went From Street Corner to Corner Office,** found Dr. Dre's net worth to be $700 million.

Believe it or not, Dre was not the richest man in hip hop that year. Sean P. Diddy Combs laid claim to the prestigious title in 2015. Diddy's worth? An estimated $735 million, which is comprised of his interests in a slew of companies including Sean John and Enyce, alkaline water brand Aquahydrate, new tequila DeLeon, and multimedia network, Revolt.

Jay Z ranked third with a fortune of $550 million. The hip hop mogul added Scandinavian streaming service Tidal to his holdings in 2015, an artist owned platform set apart by exclusive content which competes with digital music service Spotify.

I am not here to extol the financial conquests of the industry's leading players. That would be giving too much attention to "the hook" of their business acumen. I am more interested in the bigger picture. Here we have a group of men who, for the most part, hailed from humble beginnings and managed (through hard work and sound business decisions) to become titans of industry: extraordinary leaders and businessmen. At a time where it is so easy to say there is no value in hip hop, that the music is a bad influence, and that the genre breeds envy, hate and misogyny, here are four examples of artists who beat the odds, quieted the naysayers and proved that no matter where you come from or what cards you've been dealt, you can be success-ful. The critics would have us believe there is no intrinsic value in the hip hop culture. Three lives say much differently. Three lives that epitomize the **Other 99 T.Y.M.E.S.**

Where hip hop and politics intersect, therein lies the concept of **"The Other 99 T.Y.M.E.S"** You may not agree with the messages in the rap music (which critics consider controversial and bastions of anti-establishment rhetoric), but you will be hard pressed to deny its influence. As recently as 2008, Barack Obama openly embraced hip hop in his presidential campaign. Mr. Obama seized the opportu-nity to benefit from the popularity of hip hop and its most prominent entertainers by encouraging artists such as Jay Z and Sean "Diddy" Combs to campaign for him, referencing rap music in his interviews and speeches, playing rap at his events, and openly contemplating a space for hip hop in an Obama White House. It was a strategy that lat-er encouraged a new generation of potential voters to tag him as "the first hip hop President." Even performers who were well-known for penning rap lyrics interpreted as anti-status quo declared they would vote for the first time in a presidential election. Where does the **Other 99 T.Y.M.E.S.** fit into the scenario? While some were questioning the prudence of the Democratic front-runner's radical campaign meth-odology, the Center for Information and Research On Civic Learning & Engagement released a 2009 report showing estimates from the Census Current Population Survey November Supplement suggesting that the voter turnout rate among young people in 2008 was one of highest recorded.

In 2004, Sean "Diddy" Combs spearheaded the nonprofit, par-tisan organization, "Citizen Change." Its edgy, provocative slogan, "Vote or Die," was a clarion call to young potential pollsters urging

"SOL-CEO" by Kayenne Nebula

them to register to vote. Mr. Combs even set out on a three-day campaign to inform young people and minorities that voting is important and "sexy," according to a 2004 Associated Press article. Years later, Grio reported that in an interview at Revolt's music conference in Miami, Diddy revealed his thoughts about the electoral process had shifted dramatically from his position in 2004. Still, the original message was already delivered and the impact of that message (at the time Combs lent his voice in support of the voting and political process) cannot be ignored.

There are quite a few examples like the ones I just described. And for those who say, "Well, not everyone agrees that hip hop's influence on society and a new generation is always positive," I respond, fair enough. And then I remind them that they said the same thing about rock and roll, heavy metal and disco. Elvis was criticized for his gyrating hips and sexually explicit singing style. The Beatles and their extensive catalog have long been the subject of music aficionados, bloggers and historians who have delved deeply into their lyrics and found their fair share of veiled "inappropriate" lyrics. Critics often targeted Michael Jackson's suggestive choreography as being a notch below "R" rated. David Bowie assumed androgynous personae for much of what is celebrated as an "iconic" career. Yet, the role of all these artists in defining, transforming, and reinventing the music industry cannot be denied. At some point (and to varying degrees), it became as much about the creativity and the evolutionary nature of the art as the idiosyncrasies of the performer. The bigger picture tells a more compelling, progressive and lasting story. The same reasoning can be applied to hip hop. Sure, some rap lyrics do contain graphic references to drugs, sex, violence, and hate aimed at women, minorities and homosexuals. Hip hop music videos and live performances feature so-called twerking and scantily clad performers. But if you look to pop culture those same images represent empowerment: Katy Perry, J-Lo and Beyoncé are famous for their ultra-sexy costumes. However, Katy and Beyoncé, paradigms of the modern girl-power movement, are better known for their propensity to give young girls and women confidence—a voice to express themselves freely. If we focus more on what these well-known performers are wearing instead of what they are rapping about, we miss the message. Similarly, if we pay more attention to the gold chains, sagging pants and multi-million dollar cars, we miss a message. It should be more about the voice of a generation who use the medium to tell their story, reveal the struggles of poverty stricken communities, and express their discontent with the status quo. For so-called conscious rappers, it is an opportunity to rap about ways to educate others about African American history, politics and even relationships: all of which would be missed if society merely focused on the "hook" and ignored the influence. Through the omniscient lens of hindsight, most music lovers now agree that entertainers of the past broadened the music and thematic borders of their respective eras. The same, I expect, will be said of hip hop.

Ultimately, everyone is entitled to their opinion. Differing views make the world interesting. A healthy debate about any issue can be quite enlightening. The truly conscious among us know when to speak and when to reserve our opinion. If you cannot contribute a substantive thought, it is best not to prattle on mindlessly just to hear the sound of your own voice. No one can identify the uninformed until they voice their ignorance about a topic. Silence is a fool's best friend. Sadly, he is often too foolish to realize it.

12

FRONT ROW

"Someone has to die in order that the
rest of us should value life more."

THESE WORDS WERE penned by Virginia Woolf, an English writ-er and one of the foremost modernists of the twentieth century. The quote sums up my philosophy about dealing with the loss of loved ones with poignant precision.

Death is a subject I am all too familiar with—an experience most of us share. Losing someone you love is a feeling that in many ways defies comprehension. How do you make sense of a life without your mom, dad, grandparents, best friend, brother, sister or child? It's inconceivable.

The "circle of life" is a difficult concept to wrap our brains around, especially when it hits close to home. Most people are never ready. It's as if every dream you imagined, every plan you outlined, the bright future that played out in your mind's eye, all came to an abrupt end and you struggle to plant your feet on the unsettled earth beneath you. No matter how strong you think you are the pain of loss can be unbearable. When it comes to bereavement, Psychology Today explains: *everyone feels grief in their own way, but there are certain stages to the process of mourning. It starts with recognizing a loss and continues until a person eventually accepts that loss.* In this chapter, I want to address that moment when we are sitting in that "front row" dressed in black, weary from the rigors of mourning, eyes sullen and red from crying, surrounded by family and friends who bear a similar countenance of grief. As we stare helplessly (and hopelessly) at a figure bearing a faint resemblance to the person we once knew, we think back at all that we should have said, could have done and would have liked them to know. Rather than dwell on the "what ifs," we would find much greater solace in recalling the life of those we cherished and accept that their death should not overwhelm us. It serves us better to celebrate their priceless contributions to our lives (and the lives of those they touched in one way or another) and use what we've learned to heal, grow and teach. Taken in perspective, even from the loneliness and despair of the "front row," we can find the promise of life in death.

I am in no way stating that we should shrug off the grieving process. What I am advocating is that we should allow ourselves to go through its stages, learn from the soul that is no more, and reap the harvest of life that burst forth from the seeds planted!

I wrote about the loss of my parents and grandparents at great length in "Life Is Not Complicated, You Are" Some people admitted that they were surprised I described the death of my mother and father so "aloofly." A few readers suggested I lacked sentimentality or the "requisite" degree of grief and bereavement. I respected the feedback with the understanding that they did not comprehend my process any more than I would likely grasp theirs in similar circumstances. Understandably, loss in any capacity will shake you to the core. My goal is not to tell others how to feel but to simply encourage and broaden perspectives to see the **Other 99 T.Y.M.E.S.** This in no way suggests that the death of those dearest to me was not devastating. But for my personal well-being, I needed to channel that grief into a productive way of thinking or risk falling apart. That began with my understanding first that everything my loved ones taught me is invaluable—all their advice is worth its weight in gold. Were it not for the lessons they imparted (be it by words or deeds), I would not have been motivated to achieve my maximum potential. The seeds they planted became my harvest. Sometimes, as William Shakespeare wrote in his play "The Tempest," what's past is prologue. Case in point, *"Life Is Not Complicated, You Are",* my first book, would never have come to fruition were it not for the experiences my family shared. Your history can determine your future.

In his book, *The Five People You Meet in Heaven*, Mitch Albon illustrates this concept perfectly. The main character, Eddie, a wounded war veteran, is killed tragically. When he gets to "heaven," five people explain the meaning of life to him from their perspective—an experience Albon suggests everyone encounters when they cross over to the "other side." These five people revisit their connections to the deceased on earth, and, as each person recounts how they met Eddie, they reveal the secret behind the eternal question: "What is my purpose on this earth?" The answer is simple. The people we meet on our journey impact our lives. The outcome from those encounters is too important to bury under the weight of grief and regret. Think about those closest to you, the ones you respect and admire, who you turn to for advice and solace. Imagine trying to navigate the peaks and valleys of your daily routine without their assistance. Hard to conceive, right? If their role in your life proved so critical and motivational, isn't it only right that everything they taught you remain the permanent memory?

I am a perfectionist and described by many as the typical Type-A personality. The characteristic is rooted in the precedent set by my Granddaddy, the Honorable O'Neal Hunt. He would tell me often, "Baby, if you are not going to do a thing right, don't do it at all." Granted, this was (and is) not a novel concept. As far as I can tell, the

Visiting my mom and grandparents at Magnolia Cemetery in Anderson County, Texas.

philosophy dates back to biblical times. James 4:17 states, "If anyone, then, knows the good they ought to do and doesn't do it, it is sin for them." Still, what the scripture (and my grandfather's advice) may lack in originality it more than makes up for in practical application. And whether I liked what any of my elders were saying or not, whether it hurt my feelings or shamed me, I understood that they spoke from a place of awareness. Today, I am a firm believer that if you want to live with no regrets, plan your life accordingly. If you do not like to be sorry, behave in such a way you that minimizes your need to apologize. And if you are not equipped with the time, resources, dedication and passion to complete a task or chase a goal, cultivate the idea so that when conditions are right, you will be ready. Just don't let the seed (idea, training, passion, goal) die! Why risk producing a sub-par performance? Why commit to writing a mediocre book, play, screenplay or poem? Why submit an ill-prepared business plan. Once the work is out, it will forever be traced back to its origin: you. The credit is all yours, and so is the criticism, the ridicule and the disappointment. Readers, clients, and the audience are left dumbfounded by the lack of effort and vow to never entertain another project. Yes, there are extreme consequences to not doing it right from the beginning. But all is not lost. Having armed yourself with this knowledge, you can fine tune your discipline and recalibrate your commitment. Decide today to only deliver your best or nothing at all. This frame of mind is deeply engrained into my psyche and has helped order my steps toward success, thanks to my grandfather. I miss that man so much. What I would give for just one more hour with Judge Hunt. Nevertheless, I am grateful for the other "99" hours I spent with him while he was alive and willing to teach me, love me and guide me. His loss left an ache but his wisdom established a powerful legacy. The latter is my **Other 99 T.Y.M.E.S.**

My mother was a force of nature and a true warrior. She was obviously a product of her father, Judge Hunt, and her loving mother, Elnora. A day does not pass where I don't call on her strength or pray for a sign that my decisions are well thought-out and my actions are appropriate. In life, she was my best friend, my rock. In death, she remains a guardian of my conscience. I can certainly spend days wallowing in grief and despair at the loss of my mom, but to what avail? She would not have tolerated that behavior in her presence and to behave in such a manner would dishonor her memory. I apply this rationale to all aspects of my life. If there is one thing I subscribe to, it's the notion that one should always conduct him or herself with the belief that someone is watching. Reputation is, in large part, a testament to one's character. One more day with my momma would be a blessing. The 99 lessons in courage, pride, integrity and faith she imparted are my foundation.

Having sat in the front row more times than I care to remember, I realize more than ever that one should never be too busy to take a moment to express an intimate thought or share a warm or loving gesture. These are the moments that link hearts. They are the ties that bind. Never lose sight of the people who are the foundation of the future you are working to build. Nurture and reinforce that element of your life and you will surely strengthen your destiny. No act of kindness should ever be taken for granted. No deed performed out of love is ever too small to warrant a show of gratitude. Acts of affection, no matter how commonplace, still come from the heart. While there is no need for grandiose displays of thankfulness, a brief, simple word of appreciation will always serve as a gentle reminder that your roles in each other's lives are not trivialized.

I may not change the world, but I can learn from difficult lessons and share the acquired judgment accordingly. This enables me to stand resolute in a place of pride, strength, power, and yes, defiance and outrage when necessary. Moreover, I can raise my children (like my parents raised me) to understand there is so much more work to be done, and they must be part of the solution, not contribute to the problem. As John Quincy Adams, the sixth President of the United

States said, "If your actions inspire others to dream more, learn more, do more and become more, you are a leader." If and when my children, family and friends sit in the front row at my funeral, I want them to remember me, among other things, as a leader.

What will you remember most from the front row? As the tears flow and the sorrow overwhelms you, I pray you find the strength to recall the moments you smiled and laughed, the days you were comforted, and the times you learned a valuable lesson that you can carry with you and share with your loved ones. **The Other 99 T.Y.M.E.S** the love flowed as freely as your tears.

Judge O'Neal and Elnora Hunt

13

CURTAIN CALL

THE FINAL CHAPTER of each book, for whatever reason, is always the most difficult to write for me. It's as if I've come to a fork in the road and I am contemplating which path to take because this could very well be the last impression a reader walks away with. No matter what knowledge, insight, inspiration or motivation they may have extracted from the preceding chapters, this, the "Curtain Call," may frame their perspective in an entirely different way. I am sure many of you can relate. You come to the end of a project, wrap up a production, or consider the fate of a relationship, and say to yourself, "This is it! The outcome of everything I've worked for up until this moment will be determined by this final word or decision." Talk about pressure!

In typical fashion, I listened to what my instincts and my common sense told me. And of course (as I recommend to anyone who asks for my advice), acquiesced to good judgment and avoided mirroring the choices of others. The latter is typically applied because people do not want to think for themselves or are too afraid to be accountable for an unfavorable outcome. The final verse from Robert Frost's "*Road Less Traveled*" underscores this chapter's (and this book's) main premise: "Two roads diverged in the wood and I—I took the one less traveled by, and that has made all the difference."

Whenever we consider (and apply) the concept of "**The Other 99 T.Y.M.E.S**", we essentially take the road less traveled. I realize for some people it is easier to focus on the negative. It allows them room to be vulnerable, to be a victim. It invites sympathy and minimizes their responsibility. If your end game is happiness, this way of thinking is counterintuitive to contentment and peace of mind. . Happiness will never flourish in a life bereft of optimism. Marcus Aurelius wrote: *"Reject your sense of injury and the injury itself disappears."* If you choose to focus on the kindness that preceded the affront, chances are you can save a relationship. If you consider the paycheck and the insurance plan before you take offense to the boss's refusal to grant a day off, you might enjoy the job more. Life is about the choices you make. And it is in your power at all times to choose a positive perspective. Easy? Not always. Possible? Without a doubt!

That is what this book is about: each chapter is intended to shed light on the various experiences one may encounter (at home, at work, within the community) and ascertain how to train your brain to say, "Yes, this upsets me. However, yesterday this same person showed me love or kindness," and have that be the prevailing thought. When you allow the bad to outweigh the good, it exacts a taxing burden on your mind, body and soul. Many of us need to take our lives back. We need to tap into our strength, build our confidence, understand and work on our weaknesses, and control our emotions, so that when we encounter challenging situations we are armed with intelligence, logic, clarity and courage. Remember, no man, woman or situation can do anything to us we do not allow.

It's easy to constantly focus on "what went wrong." It is imperative to heed the warning signs of this behavior before we fall victim to the practice again and again. Most people dwell in that negative space because so many are conditioned to believe it is all they deserve. This line of thinking is toxic and quite frankly a fallacy. When you finally accept that you deserve better, you will demand better of (and for) yourself. You realize it is easier to forgive a fault when you acknowledge the favor. Soon, weeding out the harmful influences will become the norm not the exception.

While doing some research for 99, I happened upon a book called, *"How to be Miserable: 40 Strategies You Already Use."* Before you slam this book shut and tell the world I am a hypocrite who summed up pages of experiences that sang the praises of being positive by referencing a book that suggests the complete opposite, hear me out. Yes, the thinking (and title) appears illogical, but the objective is the same: training your brain to find the good in bad experiences. Author Randy J. Paterson, director of the Changeways clinic in Vancouver, describes it as "optimizing misery" by becoming more aware of our own detrimental habits in order to paradoxically open up new and helpful behavioral pathways. Basically, if you can isolate the things that you do that would make you feel worse — like continuing a behavior that doesn't help you — then you can similarly isolate the things that will make you feel better.

In an interview with New York Magazine, Paterson explains the reason this method is effective is that people can recognize they're not as miserable as they could possibly be. That realization can be very powerful. It can give someone a sense of hope. Both books discuss ways in which people can discipline themselves to dispel a crippling way of thinking in favor of a more constructive, self-nurturing stream of consciousness.

You own your feelings. You own your thoughts. You control both. No one has the right to any of it—to any of *you* without your permission. You wouldn't let a stranger into your bank account, your home or near your children. No one gains access to the important areas of your life if you are not absolutely sure they are there for good reason. Why not vet the strangers that want access to your heart and mind with the same vigilance?

In *"Life Is Not Complicated, You Are"*, I talk a great deal about not letting the challenges of life make you lose sight of the meaning of life. I've advanced the message to the pages of this book, just in a different style. And I don't just mean the major tragedies. I'm also referring to the little annoyances that make us wish a day would just end—a bad day at work, a minor disagreement, kids misbehaving, or an unexpected expenses. I get it. Any and all of the above could have us wishing on Monday for the moment we can say, "Thank God it's Friday!" But as my daddy used to tell me, "Do not waste your life away by wishing for days you may not even get to see." Meaning, don't lose sight of the blessing of the moment, no matter what. Look to your friends, pastor, priest, even family to encourage and support you and let you know that while things may seem insurmountable at the time, your life, your today and your moment (your **Other 99 T.Y.M.E.S**) still matters.

I read a quote that posed a question everyone should ask themselves every day: "What if you woke up today with only the things you gave thanks for yesterday?" My point is, people forget. They forget what it was like to not have something they desired and how grateful they were when (after making all kinds of promises to God and anyone that would listen) they finally received the blessing. They forget that there was someone there (maybe one person, maybe a few) who sacrificed some time or effort to get them to the next level of their lives. Folks do not stop and think that nothing in this life is owed to anyone and many neglect to appreciate that when we wake up God has granted us another day to do better and to be better. When people get happy, they forget to stay humble.

It is all about perspective. I have my obstacles and my moments too. I am definitely not perfect. My upbringing was not perfect; my life was (and is) certainly not perfect. I would never (nor should I) try to portray myself as some foremost authority on life or facing challenges. However, through my personal experiences, growth and relationships

I am intent on not allowing any aspect of my life to become meaningless or a drag. That is my hope for you: plant a seed that enables you to fully understand that each day your heart beats, that each day you take a breath and a step that each day you are able to see, smell, feel and hear, beats being underground. Moreover, for every bad day there will be 99 good ones if you choose to embrace them.

Gratitude, understanding, forgiveness, appreciation, communication and compromise.

If after the last page has been read and your favorite chapters re-read, if days after you have placed *"The Other 99 T.Y.M.E.S"* on a shelf, in your nightstand or stored the digital version on your hard drive, you gain anything, I hope it is a better understanding of how all of the above used in concert can enhance your life and strengthen your relationships.

And finally, the next time you are down on your knees pleading for whatever it is you want and the Almighty grants your wishes, remember that feeling.

ACKNOWLEDGMENTS

FIRST AND FOREMOST I would like to thank my Lord and Savior for blessing me with more than I may ever deserve and for opening doors I didn't even know existed. I thank God without ceasing for giving me the vision to realize my dreams and the motivation to continue my mission. For all this and more, I am forever grateful.

I would also like to acknowledge Tracey Wallace. Thank you for being that critical "second pair of eyes" throughout the editing process. Your patience and diligence (and of course love) helped me complete my second book. There are not enough words to express my eternal gratitude.

Liz Faublas and Million $ Pen, Ink., what can I say? We did it again! Just when I thought the bar was set impossibly high with "Life Is Not Complicated, You Are", the team at MDPI reassured me and assuaged my concerns. Moreover you made it your personal mission to deliver a work that I feel in my heart is destined to become another bestseller. Your forbearance and counsel are invaluable. Thank you for never allowing me to settle for mediocrity. Thank you for helping me paint a picture of life the world can appreciate, and hopefully benefit from.

Last but not least, I must thank my Sol-Caritas family. You all keep me grounded, humble and focused. There are times we don't see eye to eye, but realistically, what family does not have disagreements? We respect one another to see past our differences in order to achieve a common goal: success. When one of us achieves, we all prosper!

A heartfelt thank you to Lone Star College for believing in me enough to open your doors so that I could inspire the next generation to think outside the box; to be their best. To every student I have encountered (and those I have not yet met), to each social media follower or beloved fan, I appreciate your support. The feedback I have received on my first book, "Life Is Not Complicated, You Are: Turning Your Biggest Disappointments Into Your Greatest Blessings" has been nothing short of remarkable and I hope this labor of love, The 99 Other T.Y.M.E.S, is as rewarding for you as it has been for me. I encourage everyone to go forth with a positive attitude and a grateful heart and the understanding that you have the power to train your mind to enjoy serenity.

"Reality Has No Filters" image
Liz Faublas
www.lizfaublas.com

Book cover designed by:
Deonne Moore
Skylimit Graphics

Photo on front cover:
Charles Andrews
www.sol-caritas.com

Photo on back cover:
Deonne Moore
Skylimit Photography

Script on back cover:
Million$Pen, Ink.
www.milliondollarpenink.com

Made in the USA
Columbia, SC
08 September 2019